WIT(

T

WITCHCRAFT TODAY

by

GERALD B. GARDNER

*Member of one of the ancient covens of the Witch Cult
which still survive in England*

Introduction by
DR. MARGARET MURRAY
Formerly Assistant Professor in Egyptology at University College, London

With additional material
by JUDY HARROW *(coordinator)*
RONALD HUTTON, PH.D.
WREN WALKER
and TARA NELSEN

CITADEL PRESS
Kensington Publishing Corp.
www.kensingtonbooks.com

CITADEL PRESS books are published by

Kensington Publishing Corp.
850 Third Avenue
New York, NY 10022

Additional material copyright © 2004 Judy Harrow, Ronald Hutton,
    Wren Walker, and Tara Nelsen

First published in Great Britain by Rider & Company, 1954
First American paperbound edition published by Citadel Press, 1970

All Kensington titles, imprints, and distributed lines are available at special
quantity discounts for bulk purchases for sales promotions, premiums,
fund-raising, educational, or institutional use. Special book excerpts or
customized printings can also be created to fit specific needs. For details,
write or phone the office of the Kensington special sales manager.
Kensington Publishing Corp., 850 Third Avenue, New York, NY 10022,
attn: Special Sales Department, phone 1-800-221-2647.

CITADEL PRESS and the Citadel logo are Reg. U.S. Pat & TM Off.

First printing (Fiftieth Anniversary Edition): April 2004
10 9 8 7 6 5 4 3 2 1

Printed in the United States of America

Library of Congress Control Number: 2003112313
ISBN 0-8065-2593-2

CONTENTS

Some books on witchcraft—the author is permitted to write about witches "from the inside"—primitive initiations akin to witchcraft—the witch power exudes from the body, hence nudity—author's theory of an electro-magnetic field—certain rites increase clairvoyance—the author refutes Mr. Pennethorne Hughes' view that witchcraft is a cult of evil—witch rituals—witches are not disappointed perverts—their belief that their ancestors came from the east and that their paradise is in the north—ceremony to cause rebirth of the sun—the cauldron of regeneration and the dance of the wheel—the nature of the witch's circle to keep in the power—denial of the use of skulls, etc.—witches have nothing to do with the Black Mass—initiation in witchcraft develops certain powers known collectively as magic—"inside the circle they are between the worlds"—necessity for a partner.

Powers largely hereditary—their use in the Stone Ages—the Myth of the Great Mother—primitive man's wish to be born again is also that of the witches—special paradise for worshippers—witchcraft in the Old and New Testaments—witches in various places and ages—Papacy and priests treat witchcraft as a rival, like Manichees and Catharists, also Waldenses and Albigenses—identification of heathen with witches, and heretics—truth about broomsticks—the times of persecution; Mathew Hopkins and his victims—a bronze age witch in Denmark—Druid beliefs—Mexican witch cults with a native goddess—concealment of witchcraft after the coming of Christianity—the little people : pixies, fairies, or an earlier race?

The after-death realm of refreshment before rebirth—full text of the Myth of the Goddess—parallels with other beliefs—the charge read before initiation into the witch community—witchcraft is not anti-Christian—leadership by women rather than men.

landing—previous use of the same technique against
Napoleon and the Spanish Armada—the killing of 9,000,000
witches—the part played by St. Dominic—the methods of
Inquisitors; the use of torture—detailed account of tortures
used in Germany—reports of victims' utterances under
torture in Spain—Aldous Huxley's account of the torture to
death of Grandier, 1634—the author repudiates the accusation
that witches conduct a Black Mass—liberty still denied to
witches, whose object is the release of ecstasy—use of herbs
in this—the scandal of the Infamous Kiss—pacts with the
Devil and accounts of them in the *Grimoires*—pacts between
covens—contacts with other bodies in the 18th century
—numerology of witches—two meanings of the word coven
—these are smaller now—after the Norman conquest the
local lord often figured as the Devil—the use of breath control
and the ductless glands herbs and poisons—the Pope makes
surgery and witchcraft crimes—King Edward III and the
witch origin of the Order of the Garter: two covens headed
by the monarchs—the 168 letter S's on the King's robe—
untruth of the charge that witches abjure Christianity—link
with West Indian and Congo witches of today—witchcraft is
hereditary—witches believe in gods who are not omnipotent
and are pleased with man's being happy—quotation of verses
"The Witch Remembers her Last Incarnation."

long-range hypnotism—the power of determination—the author defines the anthropologist's job as investigating people's actions and beliefs, not moralists' theories—could witchcraft control the hydrogen bomb?

FOREWORD TO THE
FIFTIETH ANNIVERSARY EDITION

Witchcraft Today created a cusp, an important branching point in the history of spirituality. This single book awakened an entire way of religious thought from long, long dormancy. The contemporary Pagan renaissance, one of the fastest growing religious movements in the world, began with the book that is in your hands right now. With great good luck and Divine blessing, we may—just in time— learn again how to perceive the Sacred spark in all living things and mend our long-broken spiritual connection with Mother Earth.

Did Gerald Gardner discover, reconstruct, create, or merely popularize Witchcraft as we now practice it? Theories abound, but nobody knows for sure. Whichever theory is eventually proven correct—and I suspect the real truth lies in a synthesis of all of them— the significance of Gardner's contribution will remain: He *presented* Wicca to the modern world. Even the name we now commonly use for Witchcraft is his.

Gerald Brousseau Gardner (1884–1964) grew up with the advantage of family wealth and the disadvantage of poor health. As a result, he was mostly self-educated, left free in his youth to explore unconventional areas of knowledge, to follow the winding pathway of his own curiosity—and perhaps the leadings of the Old Gods. As an adult, he enjoyed a long career in Southeast Asia. His duties took him out of the cities and far from the European colonial enclaves. As he traveled, open-minded and receptive, among indigenous communities, he was able to experience ancient tribal rituals and spiritual practices, all still largely intact in his time.

Then, in 1936, he retired and returned to England, bringing with him all he had learned while abroad. Devoting his creativity, energy, and considerable store of knowledge to Britain's own native religion and its revival, he met a receptive community shaped by the occult interests of the early twentieth century. His path had also been prepared for by Dr. Margaret Alice Murray's theory that the infamous European Witch persecutions were actually an attempt to wipe out the last remnants of indigenous European Paganism.

Murray wrote the Witchcraft entry for the 1929 edition of the *Encyclopedia Britannica.* Her article was included in reprints of the encyclopedia until 1969. Forty years worth of English-speaking students and researchers used the *Britannica* that contained Murray's essay. This changed popular notions of Witchcraft and helped win religious tolerance for us.

In 1951, a vestige of those persecutions, the British Witchcraft Laws, were finally repealed. This made it possible for Gardner's first nonfiction work, *Witchcraft Today,* to be published three years later. Murray wrote the introduction. And with that, what had already been growing underground emerged into the sunlight and began to bud, flower, bear fruit—and propagate itself. In fact, Gardner led a coven himself for many years and trained several Priestesses to carry on his work.

Gardner's second nonfiction book, *The Meaning of Witchcraft,* followed in 1959, gathering more support. It seems to me that Gardner spent the last decade of his long and productive life as a self-appointed but very effective publicist for contemporary Wicca. He certainly welcomed the attention of journalists. His writings, interviews, and articles written about him attracted talented and devoted people, like Doreen Valiente, who would deepen, refine, and extend what Gardner shared with them.

From this point in the early 1960s on, the demographic curve turned sharply upward. Emigrants carried Wicca to the United States and Canada and throughout the English-speaking world. Other seeds were planted in continental Europe. Gardner's religion, in all its many variants, is still growing fast, now forty years after his death.

Another metamorphosis occurred on October 31, 1979. Two books were published on that one day: *Drawing Down the Moon* by Margot Adler and *The Spiral Dance* by Starhawk. Between them, these books continue to inspire us and change our ways. Both are written for bright, aware, contemporary people. The language is clear and accessible. Both shift the primary focus from spellcraft, which had been emphasized in the community, to celebration, to the joyous worship of Mother Earth.

Most important, both books make it clear, not by their content so much as by their sheer existence, that our religion is a living thing, an ongoing co-creation. What would Gardner think about this? The few remaining elders who were his students in their youth tell us that Gardner kept an open, experimental approach to religious practice and encouraged them to do the same. For that we can thank and respect Gardner, for such latitude releases our own religious creativity and wards us against sterile rote repetition. Gardner's writing, inspiring as it is, is not sacred scripture, not just some newer set of fetters for our minds and spirits.

Perhaps Gardner's religion has attracted so many because we hear the cries of our beautiful Mother Earth, now deeply wounded, still under attack and in a life-threatening crisis. The Sacred manifests in many, many ways; our special calling is to stand by Mother Gaia in Her time of need. Perhaps we are attracted to Her for reasons that we don't yet understand, reasons that will become clearer as we walk this beautiful and ancient Path.

In 1960, a biography of Gerald Gardner was published. It was credited to Jack Bracelin, then High Priest of the London Coven, but was really Gardner's own memoir, written from extensive interviews with him. (Today, the book might be published as "by Gerald Gardner with Jack Bracelin," as many ghostwritten autobiographies are.) But Wiccan elder Frederic Lamond, who was a member of the London Coven at that time, tells another version of the story. He says that Bracelin only lent his name to that book. The person who really interviewed Gardner and organized his memories was Idries Shah, the eminent Sufi teacher and writer. Shah didn't want his name on that book, perhaps because he didn't want to confuse or distract his Sufi students. As Lamond remembers it, Shah was not all that impressed with Gardner as a person; yet he made two memorable comments. He said that he had it on "good authority" that this movement would be the cornerstone of the coming age's religion, although rationally he could not see it. And he said that Gardner was driven by a force that he did not understand.*

I believe that same force moves through us still, as we work with Gardner's legacy, our own creativity, and perhaps the leadings of the Old Gods. Yes, this book is where contemporary Wicca started. That's very important. But to me, the most important thing about *Witchcraft Today*, and Gardner's other work, and all of our contributions to Wicca is to know that this is not where Witchcraft stops.

---

*Personal electronic communication, December 3, 1998.

In this edition: Besides Gardner's classic text and Margaret Murray's equally classic introduction, in this fiftieth anniversary edition, you will find five additional essays: The eminent historian, Ronald Hutton, gives us a look at Gardner's own life and times. Wren Walker, co-producer of the Witches' Voice website (www.witchvox. com), arguably the central communications hub for American Paganism right now, shares her observations about current Wiccan and Pagan doings. Graduate student Tara Nelsen looks into our possible future. I've also included two pieces of my own: an analysis of Gardner's published sources and a look at books written since his death that carry forward major themes in his work. I hope that all of these help put *Witchcraft Today* in context for the twenty-first century reader.

May this work bring good to many, harm to none, and honor to Gerald Gardner and the Ancient Gods he served.

JUDY HARROW

FOREWORD

I HAVE been told by witches in England: "Write and tell people we are not perverts. We are decent people, we only want to be left alone, but there are certain secrets that you mustn't give away." So after some argument as to exactly what I must not reveal, I am permitted to tell much that has never before been made public concerning their beliefs, their rituals and their reasons for what they do; also to emphasize that neither their present beliefs, rituals nor practices are harmful.

I write only of what takes place in the North, South, East, and West of England today in covens which I know. I have in addition shown the origin of some at least of the stories which have been told about the craft. I can only repeat the words of Lucius Apuleius in the *Metamorphoses*, xl, 23, who wrote a long account of his own initiation into the mysteries in cryptic language, saying: "I have told you things of which, although you have heard them, you cannot know the meaning."

The Museum of Magic and Witchcraft at Castleton is the only one in the world devoted to magic and witchcraft. I have the materials here to prove what I say.

I should like to get in touch with people from other covens to discuss these matters, and to hear from anyone who has any further information on the subject of witchcraft.

I wish to thank Mr. Ross Nichols, editor of Christian's *History and Practice of Magic*, for supplying me with supplementary information and for his many useful suggestions and comments.

G. B. GARDNER

Director,
The Museum of Magic and Witchcraft
The Witches' Mill,
Castletown, Isle of Man.

LIST OF ILLUSTRATIONS

INTRODUCTION

BY DR. MARGARET MURRAY

Formerly Assistant Professor in Egyptology at University College, London

IN THIS book Dr. Gardner states that he has found in various parts of England groups of people who still practise the same rites as the so-called "witches" of the Middle Ages, and that the rites are a true survival and not a mere revival copied out of books. In his easy pleasant style he gives a sketch of similar practices in ancient Greece and Rome, and his wide personal experiences in the Far East enable him to show that there are many peoples, whether in the Far East or in Great Britain, who still perform acts of worship to the Almighty Giver of Life according to ancient ritual. Though the ritual of Europe is now consonant with modern civilization, the feeling which underlies both the primitive and the civilized is the same: gratitude to the Creator and hope for the continuance of His goodness.

Personal worship may take any form, but a group of persons worshipping together always devise some form of ritual, especially when the worship takes the form of a dance. The ritual dance, whether performed as an act of worship or as the expression of a prayer, is characterized by its rhythmic action. The prayer-dance is usually for the increase of food, and therefore imitates in stylized form the movements of the animals or the growing of the plants for which increase is desired. The worship-dance is even more rhythmic than the prayer. All the movements are rhythmic, and the accompaniment is a chant or performed by percussion instruments by which the rhythm is strongly marked. The rhythmic movements, the rhythmic sounds, and the sympathy of numbers all engaged in the same actions, induce a feeling of exhilaration, which can increase to a form of intoxication. This stage is often regarded by the worshippers as a special divine favour, denoting the actual advent of the Deity into the body of the worshipper. The Bacchantes of ancient Greece induced intoxication by drinking wine, and so making themselves one with their God.

Dr. Gardner has shown in his book how much of the so-called "witchcraft" is descended from ancient rituals, and has nothing to do with spell-casting and other evil practices, but is the sincere expression of that feeling towards God which is expressed, perhaps more decorously though not more sincerely, by modern Christianity in church services. But the processional dances of the drunken Bacchantes, the wild prancings round the Holy Sepulchre as recorded by Maundrell at the end of the seventeenth century, the jumping dance of the mediaeval "witches", the solemn *zikr* of the Egyptian peasant, the whirling of the dancing dervishes, all have their origin in the desire to be "Nearer, my God, to Thee", and to show by their actions that intense gratitude which the worshippers find themselves incapable of expressing in words.

CHAPTER I

LIVING WITCHCRAFT

Some books on witchcraft—the author is permitted to write about witches "from the inside"—primitive initiations akin to witchcraft—the witch power exudes from the body, hence nudity—author's theory of an electro-magnetic field—certain rites increase clairvoyance—the author refutes Mr. Pennethorne Hughes' view that witchcraft is a cult of evil—witch rituals—witches are not disappointed perverts—their belief that their ancestors came from the east and that their paradise is in the north—ceremony to cause rebirth of the sun—the cauldron of regeneration and the dance of the wheel—the nature of the witch's circle to keep in power—denial of the use of skulls, etc.—witches have nothing to do with the Black Mass—initiation in witchcraft develops certain powers known collectively as magic—"inside the circle they are between the worlds"—necessity for a partner.

There have been many books written on witchcraft. The early ones were mostly propaganda written by the various Churches to discourage and frighten people from having any connections with what was to them a hated rival—for witchcraft is a religion. Later there were books setting out to prove that this craft had never existed. Some of these books may have been inspired or even written by witches themselves. Latterly there have been many books dealing in a scientific way with witchcraft by such writers as Dr. Margaret Murray, R. Trevor Davis, Christine Hoyle, Arne Runeberg, Pennethorne Hughes and Montague Summers. Mr. Hughes in his most scholarly book on witchcraft has, I think, clearly proved what many knew: that the Little People of the heaths, called fairies or elves at one period, were called witches in the next, but to my mind all these books have one fault. Though their authors know that witches exist, none of them seems to have asked a witch for her[1] views on the subject of witchcraft. For after all, a witch's opinions should have some value, even though they may not fit in with preconceived opinions.

Of course there are good reasons for this reticence. Recently

---

[1] Witches are as often men as women, but in English a witch is always called "she", so I will use that word, and the reader must understand it to mean either male or female.

I was talking to a very learned Continental professor who was writing up some witch trials of two hundred years ago, and he told me that he had obtained much information from witches. But, though invited, he had been afraid to go to their meetings. Religious feeling was very strong in his country and if it were known that he was in communication with witches he would be in danger of losing his professorship. Moreover, witches are shy people, and publicity is the last thing they want. I asked the first one I knew: "Why do you keep all this wonderful knowledge secret? There is no persecution nowadays." I was told: "Isn't there? If it were known in the village what I am, every time anyone's chickens died, every time a child became sick, I should be blamed. Witchcraft doesn't pay for broken windows!"[1]

Now I am an anthropologist, and it is agreed that an anthropologist's job is to investigate what people do and believe, and not what other people say they should do and believe. It is also part of his task to read as many writings as possible on the matter he is investigating, though not accepting such writings uncritically, especially when in conflict with the evidence as he finds it. Anthropologists may draw their own conclusions and advance any theories of their own, but they must make it clear that these are their own conclusions and their own theories and not proven facts; and this is the method I propose to adopt. In dealing with native races one records their folklore, the stories and religious rites on which they base their beliefs and actions. So why not do the same with English witches?

I must first explain why I claim to speak of things not generally known. I have been interested in magic and kindred subjects all my life, and have made a collection of magical instruments and charms. These studies led me to spiritualist and other societies, and I met some people who claimed to have known me in a past life. Here I must say that, though I believe in reincarnation, as most people do who have lived in the East, I do not remember any past lives, albeit I have had curious experiences. I only wish I did. Anyhow, I soon found myself in the circle and took the usual oaths of secrecy which bound me not to reveal any secrets of the cult. But, as it is a dying cult, I thought it was a pity that all the knowledge

[1] *See* Note 1 (page 159).

should be lost, so in the end I was permitted to write, as fiction, something of what a witch believes in the novel *High Magic's Aid*.[1] This present volume has the same purpose, but deals with the subject in a factual way.

Many people ask me how I can believe in magic. If I explain what I believe magic to be, I go a long way towards an answer. My view is that it is simply the use of some abnormal faculty. It is a recognized fact that such faculties exist. So-called calculating boys are famous, and very many people have the faculty under hypnotic control to calculate time most accurately. While asleep they are ordered to do something at, say, the end of a million seconds; they will know nothing of this order in their normal state, but their inner consciousness calculates it and at the end of the millionth second they obey the order without knowing why. Try to calculate a million seconds in your waking state, and say when it is up, without a watch, and you will see what I mean. The powers used are utterly unlike any mental powers we know. And exercising them is normally impossible. So, if there are some people with some abnormal powers, why should there not be other people who have other forms of abnormal powers and unusual ways of inducing them?

I am continually being asked various questions regarding the witch cult, and I can only answer: Nearly all primitive people had initiation ceremonies and some of these were initiation into priesthoods, into magic powers, secret societies and mysteries. They were usually regarded as necessary for the welfare of the tribe as well as for the individual. They usually included purification and some test of courage and fortitude—often severe and painful—terrorization, instruction in tribal lore, in sexual knowledge, in the making of charms, and in religious and magical matters generally, and often a ritual of death and resurrection.

Now I did not cause the primitive people to do these things; I simply hold that witches, being in many cases the descendants of primitive people, do in fact do many of them. So when people, for example, ask me: "Why do you say that witches work naked?" I can only say: "Because they do." "Why?" is another question, the easy reply being that their ritual tells them they must. Another is that their practices are the remnants of a Stone Age

[1] Published by Michael Houghton, 49 Museum Street, London, W.C.1.

religion and they keep to their old ways. There is also the Church's explanation: "Because witches are inherently wicked." But I think the witches' own explanation is the best: "Because only in that way can we obtain power."

Witches are taught and believe that the power resides within their bodies which they can release in various ways, the simplest being dancing round in a circle, singing or shouting, to induce a frenzy; this power they believe exudes from their bodies, clothes impeding its release. In dealing with such matters it is, of course, difficult to say how much is real and how much imagination.

As in the case of dowsing, if a man believes that when insulated from the ground by rubber insoles he cannot find water, this belief inhibits him, even though the insoles contain no rubber, whilst wearing insoles made of rubber—though he didn't know it—he can find water, as many experiments prove.

It is easy to imagine that a witch who firmly believes that it is essential to be naked could not whip up the final effort to attain the ecstasy without being naked. Another, however, who did not share this belief might, though partially clothed, exert sufficient energy to force power through her face, shoulders, arms and legs, to produce some result; but who can say that she could not have produced twice the power with half the effort had she been in the traditional nakedness? All we can be sure of is that in ancient times it was recognized that witches did so and even journeyed to their meetings in that costume; but in later times the Church, and more especially the Puritans, tried to hush this up and invented the story of the foul old woman on a broomstick, to replace the story told at so many witch trials of wild dances in the moonlight by beautiful young witches.

Personally I am inclined to believe that while allowing for imagination there is something in the witches' belief. I think that there is something in the nature of an electro-magnetic field surrounding all living bodies, and that this is what is seen by some people who call it the aura. I can sometimes see it myself, but only on bare flesh, so clothes evidently obstruct its functioning; this, however, is simply my own private belief. I think a witch by her formulae stimulates it, or possibly creates more of it. They say that witches by constant practice can train their wills to blend this nerve force, or whatever it is, and that their united wills can project this as a beam of force, or that they can use it in other ways to gain clairvoyance, or even to release the astral body. These practices include increasing and quickening the blood supply, or in other cases slowing it down, as well as the use of will-power; so it is reasonable to believe that it does have some effect. I am not stating that it does. I only record the fact that they attempt these effects, and believe that sometimes they succeed. The only way to find the truth or falsity of this would be to experiment. (I should think that slips or Bikinis could be worn without unduly causing loss of power. It would be interesting to try the effect of one team in the traditional nude and one in Bikinis.) At the same time one might heed the witches' dictum: "You must be this way always in the rites, 'tis the command of the Goddess." You must be this way so that it becomes second nature; you are no longer naked, you are simply natural and comfortable.

The cult, whether in England or elsewhere, starts with several advantages. First, it usually obtains recruits very young and slowly trains them so that they come to have the sense of mystery and wonder, the knowledge that they have an age-old tradition behind them. They have probably seen things happen and know they can happen again: instead of mere curiosity and a pious belief that "something may happen", inhibited by an unacknowledged but firm belief that "it will never happen to me".

What it comes to, then, is this: certain people were born with clairvoyant powers. They discovered that certain rites and processes increased these powers, thus they became useful to the community. They performed these rites, and obtained benefits, and being lucky and successful were looked at with envy and dislike by others, and so they began to perform their rites in secret. Power which can be used for good can be used for evil, and they were tempted perhaps to use this power against their opponents, and thus become more unpopular. As a result calamities would be laid at their doors, and people would be tortured till they confessed to causing them. And who can blame the children of some of those thus tortured to death for making a wax image of their oppressors?

That, in brief, is the truth about witchcraft. In mid-Victorian days it would have been shocking, but in these days of nudist clubs is it so very terrible? It seems to me more or less like a family party trying a scientific experiment according to the text-book.

I should like at this stage to deal with the view, not infrequently held, that witchcraft has connections with diabolism. Mr. Summers himself appears to think the question is settled because the Roman Catholic Church said the cult was diabolic, and Mr. Pennethorne Hughes's book also gives the impression that witchcraft is a cult of evil. Mr. Hughes says (page 128):

"As the cult declined, any sort of common practice must have been lost, until by the nineteenth century the indoor practitioners of selfconscious diabolism merely conducted the Black Mass of inverted Catholicism. At the time of the trials there was clearly some sort of formal service quite apart from the crescendo of the fertility dance. It would, in a Catholic Age, be very like the known pageantry of the Church's own celebrations, with candles, vestments and a parody of the sacrament. It might be conducted by an unfrocked priest using hosts with the devil's name stamped on them instead of Jesus, and the defiling of the Crucifix—to insult Christians and please the Devil. The Devil himself received praise and homage. A liturgy of evil would be repeated, there would be a mock sermon and absolution made with the left hand and an inverted cross."

Those who attended these meetings he dismisses in the following way (page 131):

"Some were perhaps dissipated perverts and had shame or guilty pride; some were just members of a primitive stock, already disappearing, but still following the ways of their fathers, knowing the Church disapproved yet finding physical and psychological satisfaction. Some were ecstatic. 'The Sabbat,' said one, 'is the true Paradise.' "

Mr. Hughes does not say why he thinks they should have given up their own rites, which were made for a definite purpose and which produced definite results simply to parody those of an alien faith. I have attended many of these cult rites, and I declare that most of what he says is simply not true. There may be a fertility dance, but the other rites are simple, and with a purpose, and in no way resemble those of the Roman Catholic or any other Church that I know. True, sometimes there is a short ceremony when cakes and wine are blessed and eaten. (They tell me that in the old days mead or ale was often used.) This may be in imitation of the early Christian Agape, the Love Feast, but there is no suggestion that the cakes turn into flesh and blood. The ceremony is simply intended as a short repast, though it is definitely religious.

The priestess usually presides. Candles are used, one to read the book by and others set round the circle. This does not in any way resemble the practice of any other religious sect I know. I do not think that can be called "imitation of the Church's pageantry".

There are no crucifixes, inverted or otherwise, no sermons, mock or otherwise, and no absolution or hosts save for the cake and wine mentioned. Incense is used, but this has a practical purpose. There is no praise or homage to the Devil, no liturgy, evil or otherwise, nothing is said backwards, and there are no gestures with the left hand; in fact with the exception that it is a religious service and all religious services resemble one another, the rites are not in any way an imitation of anything I have ever seen. I do not say there have never been diabolists. I only say that, as far as I know, witches do not do the things of which they have been accused, and knowing what I do of their religion and practices I do not think they ever did.

Naturally it is impossible to speak for all of them. I have seen in print that priests and clergymen have been convicted of every crime there is in British law, and in the Isle of Man priests have been convicted of singing psalms of destruction against people (vide the Isle of Man N. M. & A. Soc. Proceedings, vol. v, 1946), which is a new crime to me at least; but this does not mean that the majority of priests and clergymen are criminals. Nor do I think it fair to call witches disappointed perverts. They may truly be said to be followers of a primitive religion, already disappearing; they are following the ways of their fathers, knowing the Church disapproves of their practices, but finding physical and psychological satisfaction. And cannot the same be said of the Buddhists or Shintoists? They have ancient, and to them good rites, and they are not in the least concerned if others disapprove. All that matters to them is, are they on the Path? I have learnt tolerance in the many years I spent in the East and if anyone finds true paradise in the Buddhist rites, the Sabbat, or the Mass, I am well content.

If I were permitted to disclose all their rituals, I think it would be easy to prove that witches are not diabolists; but the oaths are solemn and the witches are my friends. I would not hurt their feelings. They have secrets which to them are sacred. They have good reason for this secrecy. I am, however, permitted to give one sample of their rites. It tells little, for, apart from the rites, they themselves know little. For one reason or another they keep the names of their god and goddess a secret. To them the cult has existed unchanged from the beginning of time, though there is also a vague notion that the old people came from the East, possibly as a result of the Christian belief that the East is the holy place whence everything came. In this connection it should be noted that witches start in the East when forming the circle, and the representative of the god or goddess usually stands in the East. This may simply be because the sun and moon rise in the East, because of the position of the altar, or for some unknown reason, since actually the main invocations are towards the North. I have been given no reason for this; but I have an idea that in the old days they thought their paradise lay in the North, as they hold that the Northern Lights are the lights of their paradise, though this is usually thought of as being underground, or in a hollow hill. It is worth noting, too, that Scandinavian mythology makes the North the dwelling-place of the gods, and that in Gaelic myth the South, often camouflaged as "Spain", is evil or hell. Presumably, therefore, its opposite, the North, is paradise.

I have seen one very interesting ceremony: the Cauldron of Regeneration and the Dance of the Wheel, or Yule, to cause the sun to be reborn, or summer to return. This in theory should be on December 22, but nowadays it is held on the nearest day to that date that is convenient for the members. The ceremony starts in the usual way. The circle is cast and purified, the celebrants also being purified in the usual manner, and the ordinary business of the cult is done. Then the small ceremony is performed (sometimes called "Drawing down the Moon") so that the High Priestess is regarded as the incarnation of the goddess.

The Cakes and Wine ceremony follows. Then a cauldron (or something to represent one) is placed in the middle of the circle, spirit is put in and ignited. Various leaves, etc., are cast in. Then the Priestess stands by it in the pentacle (goddess) position. The High Priest stands on the opposite side of the cauldron, leading the chant. The others stand round in a circle with torches. They are lighted at the burning cauldron and they dance round in the "sunwise" direction, i.e. clockwise. The chant I heard was as follows, but others are sometimes used:

> "Queen of the Moon, Queen of the Sun,
> Queen of the Heavens, Queen of the Stars,
> Queen of the Waters, Queen of the Earth
> Bring to us the Child of Promise![1]
>
> It is the great mother who giveth birth to him,
> It is the Lord of Life who is born again.
> Darkness and tears are set aside
> When the Sun shall come up early.
>
> Golden Sun of the Mountains,
> Illumine the Land, Light up the World,
> Illumine the Seas and the Rivers,
> Sorrows be laid, Joy to the World.
>
> Blessed be the Great Goddess,
> Without beginning, without end,
> Everlasting to eternity.
> I.O. EVO.HE Blessed Be."

They dance round furiously, crying:

> "I.O. EVO.HE
> Blessed Be I.O. EVO.HE Blessed Be."

Sometimes couples join hands and jump over the blazing cauldron, as I have seen for myself. When the fire had burnt itself out the Priestess led the usual dances. This was followed by a feast.

Is there anything very wicked or awful in all this? If it were

[1] The Sun, thought of as being reborn.

performed in a church, omitting the word goddess or substituting the name of a saint, would anyone object?

Other rites I am forbidden to give because they are definitely magical, though otherwise they are no more harmful than this. But they do not wish it to be known how they raise power. The dances that follow are more like children's games than modern dances—they might be called boisterous and noisy, with much laughter. In fact, they *are* more or less children's games performed by grown-ups, and like children's games they have a story, or are done for a certain definite purpose other than mere enjoyment.

I am also permitted to tell for the first time in print the true reason why the important thing in all their ceremonies is "Casting the Circle". They are taught that the circle is "between the worlds", that is, between this world and the next, the dominions of the gods.

The circle such as it is shown in pictures may or may not be used. It is most convenient to mark it with chalk, paint or otherwise, to show where it is; but marks on the carpet may be utilized. Furniture may be placed to indicate the bounds. The only circle that matters is the one drawn before every ceremony with either a duly consecrated Magic Sword or a Knife, the latter being the Witches' Athame or Black-Hilted Knife, with magic signs on the hilt, and this is most generally used. The circle is usually nine feet in diameter, unless made for some very special purpose. There are two outer circles, each six inches apart, so the third circle has a diameter of eleven feet. When drawn, this circle is carefully purified, as also are all who celebrate the rites. Witches attach great importance to this, for within the circle is the gods' domain.

It is necessary to distinguish this clearly from the work of the magician or sorcerer, who draws a circle on the ground and fortifies it with mighty words of power and summons (or attempts to summon) spirits and demons to do his bidding, the circle being to prevent them from doing him harm, and he dare not leave it.

The Witches' Circle, on the other hand, is to *keep in* the power which they believe they can raise from their own bodies and to prevent it from being dissipated before they can mould it to their own will. They can and do step in and out if they wish to, but this involves some loss of power, so they avoid doing so as much as possible.

People try to make me say that in the rites skulls and other repulsive things are used. I have never seen such things; but they tell me that in the old days sometimes, when the High Priest was not present, a skull and crossbones was used to represent the god, death and resurrection (or reincarnation). Nowadays the High Priestess stands in a position representing the skull and crossbones, or death, and moves to another position, a pentacle, representing resurrection, during the rites. I expect the old village herbalist type of witch may have used skulls and bones and other things to impress people because they were expected to. They were good psychologists, and if a patient was convinced that only a nasty-tasting medicine would do him good, then the witches' draught was sure to taste horrible—and consequently it cured. If the people firmly believed that mumbo-jumbo with skulls and bones gave the witch power to cure or kill, then the skulls and bones would be there, for witches are consummate leg-pullers; they are taught it as part of their stock-in-trade.

It is often thought that the performance of the Black Mass is part of the tradition of witchcraft; but to use the late Dr. Joad's words, "it all depends on what you mean" by the Black Mass. I understand it to be a blasphemous parody of the Catholic Mass. I have neither seen nor heard of this in connection with the cult, and I do not believe it ever existed as one of their rites. Rites are performed for certain purposes. These take time, but when they are finished the assembly have a little meal, then dance and enjoy themselves. They have no time or inclination for indulging in blasphemy. Has anyone ever heard of people wasting time in troubling themselves to go through a parody of a Buddhist or Mohammedan rite?

Another thing I have always understood is that to perform a Black Mass you needed a Catholic priest who would perform a valid transubstantiation: God so present in the Host would then be desecrated. Unless it were a valid communion there could be no desecration. I should be surprised to find a Catholic priest among witches nowadays, though in the past many are said to have been members of the cult. It has been suggested that witches did not really celebrate the **Black Mass** but that people become witches by obtaining hosts, either by stealing the reserved sacrament from the churches or by receiving the communion and keeping it under their tongues and then putting it in their pockets; this was then taken to the rites and desecrated. During my lifetime there has been much trouble because priests and missionaries have destroyed or desecrated figures of heathen gods, and I also believe that some eminent Nonconformist churchmen have obtained consecrated hosts and held them up to ridicule. But I have never heard that so doing made them witches, and I do not think that witches ever do it or did it. On the other hand, there have been many instances of consecrated hosts being made use of in unorthodox ways by people who were not witches; to stop fires or volcanic eruptions, for instance, or to wear round the neck as personal charms, to bring good fortune, avert evil and, especially, to checkmate attacks by vampires; but all this was done by believers. A witch would not do these things, since she believes she can fabricate much more powerful charms of her own.

I believe, however, that sometimes the Black Mass *is* performed. Once I doubted it; but in February, 1952, I was in Rome and was told that some unfrocked priests and nuns celebrated it at times. My informants said they could arrange for me to see it done properly by these unfrocked priests and nuns, but that it would cost me about £20; I had not enough foreign exchange or else I would have gone, so as to settle the question to my own satisfaction. I think it was probably a show put on for the tourists, though I was assured by responsible people that it was not.

In short, I believe that people may perform Black Masses at times for a thrill, or with evil intent; but I do not believe that these people are witches, or know anything about witchcraft. Incidentally, I met more than one witch in Rome, though witches have to keep underground, and they knew nothing of this Black Mass.

Being initiated into the witch cult does not give a witch supernatural powers as I reckon them, but instructions are given, in rather veiled terms, in processes which develop various clairvoyant and other powers, in those who naturally possess them slightly. If they have none they can create none. Some of these powers are akin to magnetism, mesmerism and suggestion, and depend on the possibility of forming a sort of human battery, as it were, of combined human wills working together to influence persons or events at a distance. They have instructions in how to learn to do this by practice. It would take many people a long time, if I understand the directions aright. If these arts were more generally practised nowadays, we should call most of them spiritualism, mesmerism, suggestion, E.S.P., Yoga or perhaps Christian Science; to a witch it is all MAGIC, and magic is the art of getting results. To do this certain processes are necessary and the rites are such that these processes may be used. In other words, they condition you. This is the secret of the cult.

I do not say that these processes are the only way to develop these powers. I presume that professional clairvoyants, for instance, have some method of teaching or training to bring out the powers which they naturally possess. It is possible that their method may be superior to that of witchcraft; possibly they know the witches' system and all the teaching it involves and keep it as a trade secret. Witches are also taught that in some mysterious way "inside the circle they are between the worlds" (this world and the next), and "that which happens between the worlds does not concern this world". To form this battery of wills, male and female intelligences are necessary in couples. In practice these are usually husband and wife, but there are younger people who often form attachments which usually end in marriage. There are also, of course, some unattached people, or some whose respective spouses are for some reason or other not members of the cult. I have heard fierce purists declare that no married man or woman should belong to, or attend, any club or society to which their respective partners did not also belong; but such strict views are not part of witchcraft.

Witchcraft was, and is, not a cult for everybody. Unless you have an attraction towards the occult, a sense of wonder, a feeling that you can slip for a few minutes out of this world into the other world of faery, it is of no use to you. By it you can obtain peace, the soothing of jangled nerves and many other benefits, just from the companionship, but to obtain the more fundamental effects you must attempt to develop any occult power you may have. But it is no use trying to develop these powers unless you have time and a suitable partner, and it is no place to take your maiden aunt, even if she is romantic; for witches, being realists, have few inhibitions and if they want to produce certain effects they do so in the most simple way. Although most of their activities have been for good, or have at least been harmless, certain aspects gave the Church in England and the Puritans the chance to accuse them of all kinds of immoralities, Devil-worship and cannibalism, as I have shown. Torture sometimes made poor wretches confess to these impossibilities, in order to lead the questioning away from the truth. The fact that their god had horns caused him to be identified with the Devil. The fact that witches were often people of some property worth looting supplied the incentive; rack and branding iron did the rest. Christian fear and Christian fire prevailed. The few remaining members of the cult dived underground and have remained secretive ever since. They are happy practising their lovely old rites. They do not want converts: converts mean talk: talk means bother and semi-persecution. All they desire is peace.

CHAPTER II

THERE HAVE BEEN WITCHES IN ALL AGES

Powers largely hereditary—their use in the Stone Ages—the Myth of the Great Mother—primitive man's wish to be born again is also that of the witches—special paradise for worshippers—witchcraft in the Old and New Testaments—witches in various places and ages—Papacy and priests treat witchcraft as a rival, like Manichees and Catharists, also Waldenses and Albigenses—identification of heathen with witches, and heretics—truth about broomsticks—the times of persecution; Mathew Hopkins and his victims—a bronze age witch in Denmark—Druid beliefs—Mexican witch cults with a native goddess—concealment of witchcraft after the coming of Christianity—the little people: pixies, fairies, or an earlier race?

THERE have been witches in all ages and countries. That is, there have been men and women who have had a knowledge of cures, philtres, charms and love potions and at times poisons. Sometimes it was believed they could affect the weather, bringing rain or drought. At times they were hated, at times they were loved; at times they were highly honoured, at times persecuted. They claimed to be, or were credited with being, in communication with the world of spirits, the dead, and sometimes with the lesser gods. It was generally thought that their powers were hereditary, or that the craft was apt to run in families. People went to them whenever they were in trouble for cures, good crops, good fishing or whatever their need was. They were, in fact, the priestesses or representatives of the little gods, who because they were little would bother to listen to the troubles of little people. They are usually thought of as wild dancers, as being "not too strict".

In the Stone Ages man's chief wants were good crops, good hunting, good fishing, increase in flocks and herds and many children to make the tribe strong. It became the witches' duty to perform rites to obtain these things. This was probably a matriarchal age, when man was the hunter and woman stayed at home making medicine and magic. Historically, the matriarchal period has been tentatively dated from the middle of the ninth to the middle of the seventh millennium B.C., during which time caves, trees, the moon and stars all seem to have been reverenced as female emblems. So the myth of the Great Mother came into existence and woman was her priestess. Probably at the same time the men had a hunter's god, who presided over the animals. Later, perhaps, came the idea of a future life and thoughts of the next world as being an unhappy place unless you could attain to the abode of the gods, a sort of paradise. This was thought of as a place of rest and refreshment where one would grow young again ready for reincarnation on earth.

Primitive man feared to be born again outside his own tribe, so his ritual prayers to his god were that he might be born again in the same place and at the same time as his loved ones, and that he might remember and love them again. The god who rules this paradise must, I think, have been Death, but somehow he is identified with the hunting god and wears his horns. This god of death and hunting, or his representative, seems at one time to have taken the lead in the cult, and man became the master. But it is emphasized that because of her beauty, sweetness and goodness, man places woman, as the god placed the goddess, in the chief place, so that woman is dominant in the cult practice.

What probably happened was this: there was an organized tribal religion, with a male tribal god, and an order of priestesses and their husbands who looked after the magic. The chief priest of the tribal cult was dominant when he attended their meetings, but in his absence the priestess ruled. My witches speak of him as god of "Death and what lies beyond": by this they not only mean the life in the next world but resurrection (or reincarnation). He rules a sort of happy hunting ground, where ordinary folk go and forgather with like-minded people; it may be pleasant or unpleasant according to your nature. According to your merits you may be reincarnated in time, and take your chance where and among whom this takes place; but the god has a special paradise for his worshippers, who have conditioned their bodies and natures on earth, who enjoy special advantages and are prepared more swiftly for reincarnation which is done by the power of the goddess in such circumstances as to ensure that you will be reborn into your own tribe again. This is taken nowadays to mean into witch circles. It would seem to involve an un-ending series of reincarnations; but I am told that in time you may become one of the mighty ones, who are also called the mighty dead. I can learn nothing about them, but they seem to be like demigods—or one might call them saints.

At a later time there were, perhaps, other reasons why women may have been dominant in the cult practice, though, as I point out later, there are quite as many men among witches as women. The Bible tells us of the poor persecuted Witch of Endor, working in secret when all other witches had been driven out of the land. It also tells us of Huldah the Sorceress, living in state in Jerusalem, consulted by the King on high points of religion when the High Priest himself could not answer. The unfortunate consequence of the low position of woman in the Middle Ages, when it was against the general tradition of the Church to try and improve her status, or raise it to what it was in pre-Christian times, should be remembered. So the Church fulminated against Paracelsus when he wrote a book in praise of women, calling him a "woman worshipper". As Mr. Hughes says:

"This meant that many women resented this subjugation, and a secret religion, where woman was important and which made sexual activity a proud mystery instead of a drudgery, was made. This religion also served as a psychological Cave of Adullam for emotional women, repressed women, masculine women, and those suffering from personal disappointment, or from nervous maladjustment which had not been resolved by the local resources of the Church."

The individual motives which persuaded a person to become a witch, other than those to whom witchcraft was an old religion, must have been fairly complicated. As other cults have found, although the practices gave rest, peace, and joy to many, some of their recruits were rather an embarrassment, and as legions of spies may have tried to gain entrance to betray them, from an early date recruits were admitted only from people who were of the blood; that is, from a witch family. The various rituals of worship, secrets of herbal lore, and the Great Secret of what they call magic, have been handed down to what has become more or less a family secret society.

In Palestine and other countries there are two kinds of witches: the ignorant herbalist and charm-seller, and the witch who is a descendant of a line of priests and priestesses of an old and probably Stone Age religion, who have been initiated in a certain way (received into the circle) and become the recipients of certain ancient learning.

At times the Church ignored the witch; but when the Papacy became firmly established the priests treated the cult as a hated rival and tried to persecute it out of existence. The Puritans also took up the work with glee, and between them they practically succeeded.

From the eleventh century onwards the Church had a number of dangerous rivals. The Manichean doctrines were widespread in southern Europe; these had many different sects but they lived peacefully side by side. They were largely synonymous with the Catharists. They had their own bishops and deacons, and had great reverence for their "Perfects"—initiated persons who were regarded as almost divine. They prostrated themselves before them, saying: "Benedicite." The Perfects also adored each other, though this adoration was not directed towards themselves but towards the Holy Spirit who had descended upon them. The Church charged the Catharists with believing and teaching that they could freely indulge in all kinds of pleasures or debaucheries until they entered the circle of Perfects; that their souls wandered about from one creature to another (reincarnation) until they became Perfects, and then ascended to heaven at death. They were also charged with persuading people not to give money to the Church.

There were similar sects known as Waldenses and Albigenses. We know practically only what the Church tells us about them and she makes identical charges against them all, with witchcraft thrown in for good measure. Crusades were organized, very large numbers of people were massacred, the sects disappeared underground, and the persecution was switched to the heathens, the People of the Heaths, who carried on the old religion. Seemingly it was taken for granted that all heathens were heretics and witches, and that all witches were automatically heretics.

As part of this campaign all sorts of false ideas were spread until the popular notion of a witch became that of the common definition: "a witch is an old woman who flies through the air on a broomstick". Now no witch ever flew through the air on a broomstick or on anything else, at least not until aeroplanes

came in. There is indeed a fertility charm to bring good crops
which is performed by riding on a pole, or broom, as a hobby-
horse. Doubtless ancient witches practised this rite, leaping high
to make the crops grow. In early trials witnesses speak of seeing
the accused riding on poles, or brooms, across the fields (not
through the air), and this was often accepted as the evidence
that they were practising fertility magic, which became a penal
offence. In the Castletown Museum there is one of these poles for
riding, the head being carved in the shape of a phallus to bring
fertility.

In the Isle of Man in 1617 a woman was seen trying to obtain
a good harvest in this way. She was tried, convicted and burnt
to death in the market place. There was plenty of evidence that
she was alone in her fertility-making attempt, but her young son
was burnt with her, for it was well known that children were
usually initiated when they were quite young. This just shows
what a myth the old witch story is. The children were made
witches when they were young, therefore witches were of all
ages. Indeed, reports of the trials often include such items as
these: "Convicted and burned, two witches, girls of 16, both
young and damnably pretty."

When practically all the witches were driven underground it
is estimated that nine million people were tortured to death
during the persecution in Europe; any old woman who then
lived by herself, and who was a nuisance or unpopular, was
liable to be accused, especially if she kept a pet and talked to it,
or talked to herself, as so many lonely old women are apt to do.
Such an accusation meant fun for the mob, stripping, pricking,
ducking and so on, as well as good pay for the professional witch-
finder. In England, Mathew Hopkins made a very good thing out
of this. He went about finding out who was unpopular with the
Puritan régime and tortured them to get confessions; he also
picked up any unpopular old women on the way and had them
executed. He was paid a pound a head for all convictions; and
this represents considerably more nowadays. There were many
others who did the same. Pricking and swimming ensured
a charge and the offenders could be tortured at will. Often they
confessed, for hanging, or even half an hour's burning, was better
than weeks of continual torture. In this way the old witch notion

became generally believed. It is unlikely that any of these old women were real witches, that is, that they had been initiated into the circle; but doubtless some of them knew many old wives' cures.

To go back to a much earlier time, Arne Runeberg tells us of the grave of a witch of the Bronze Age found in Denmark. Among costly swords and gold jewellery this female magician had a bronze bowl containing the following. We add their uses in modern days:

1. The claw of a lynx. Used today as medicine and as an amulet.
2. Bones of a weasel. Weasel's skin is still used as a remedy against all sorts of diseases in animals.
3. Vertebrae of snakes. Pulverized snake-skin and snake joints are still used as medicine for sick animals.
4. Horses' teeth, torn out and broken in pieces. These are used today, hung round children's necks to make their teeth grow strong.
5. Twig of rowan. Rowan twigs are used today as charms, etc.
6. Charcoal of aspen. Charcoal of an aspen tree set on fire by lightning is still a medicine of special force.
7. An iron knife blade and a bronze thread. Steel has a great force, especially if it has an edge.
8. Two pieces of iron pyrites. Every sort of ill-willing is cured by striking fire with pyrites over the patient.
9. A number of pieces of small bone, pebbles and clay.

Thus it would seem that old ideas continued for a long time. This Bronze Age witch was evidently an important person, and the cures she used are practically the same as Danish folk charms today, so it is at least conceivable that other knowledge might also survive. The Scandinavian Sagas show striking resemblances to the European witch beliefs of today, riding on staffs, wild waving hair, sending the soul out of the body, changing of shapes and many other things. The religion of the ancient Celts was quite different from the Scandinavian, but the Druids were priests, doctors and teachers causing good or bad harvests, making women and cattle fruitful, and causing a magic (hypnotic) sleep.

The accounts of both Latin and Gaelic writers give us a fair idea of the high estimation the natives had for their Druids, and both in Gaul and in Ireland it was believed that the cult originated in Britain. So they sent their "theological students" there to learn its doctrines from the purest source. Pliny the Elder tells us that Britain "might have taught magic to Persia". We know little of their teachings, but they believed in reincarnation. Caesar tells us they held the following belief: "Souls are not annihilated, but pass after death from one body to another . . . by this teaching men are much encouraged to valour, through disregarding the fear of death." This was the usual belief, as the hero Cuchulain was urged by the men of Ulster to marry, because they did not wish to lose so great a warrior to the tribe, and knew that he would be reborn again among his descendants. The Book of the Dun Cow tells us that the famous Fin mac Coul was reborn in Ulster in the person of King Mongan, two hundred years after his death.

There was also a class of diviners called Druidesses and mentioned by Caesar in his *De Bello Gallico*, who were looked on as even more ancient than the Druids; they were shape-changers and seem to have had all the characteristics of witches. They made rain by sprinkling water over or beside nude virgins. Christians accused them of "baptizing" children into heathenism. Their association could only be entered by initiation, and learning and practising their secret lore. Their magic power was much feared by early Christians, who ascribed it to the Devil.

If we only knew really what the Druids believed and taught, whether there was only one form of belief and whether they had various sects among them, it would be easier to say whether there was any connection or not with witchcraft. The latter may have been purely orthodox, thought of as extremely high or ultra low in type, the fanciful religion of a lot of women, a vile heresy, or simply the religion of the natives that no decent person might have anything to do with. It is quite possible that it was several of these things at different times and in different parts of the country. My own impression is that it was thought of as the religion of the pre-Celtic peoples with their own gods, and the Druids thought it good and right that people should have and worship their own gods. But slowly Celtic ideas crept in. I think the myth of the goddess is clearly such. That is, a minor Celtic goddess crept in and by her beauty and sweetness wrought great changes in a primitive hunters' cult. This is simply a wild guess on my part, and I give these personal opinions because I am not permitted to detail the rites and prayers on which I base them. And, of course, the reverse may have happened; it may have been an orthodox Celtic cult into which more primitive beliefs and practices infiltrated during the crash following the Roman invasion and the introduction of Christianity, and we must take into account the effects of the Greek and Roman mystery religions. After the Saxon invasion there probably was an influx of Roman-British nominal Christians, who entered the witch-cult thinking that the invasion was a punishment for deserting the old gods, and that the witches' gods were the true ancient gods with other names.

It may only be a coincidence that in Mexico there was a witch cult much resembling that in Europe, which existed from pre-Columbian times. They had a goddess, or witch queen, always represented as naked and carrying or riding a broom. (This represented cleanliness or ritual purity in Mexico.) The European witch laid great stress on cleanliness and purity.

At their meetings the women were always naked, but wore either a necklace or a short cape (women witches in Europe lay great stress on necklaces). In Mexico the men wore a skin flap fore and aft, like the Irish witches, but removed this for certain ceremonies. Indians did not kiss, but gave a caress of welcome. They usually worked within small chambers, with wall paintings, which confined the power raised, just as witches use a circle for the same purpose.

Though it is not impossible that there was some intercourse across the Atlantic before Columbus, I think it is more likely that similar causes produced similar effects on both sides of the world.

It may seem impossible to some that any cult could have preserved its identity and teachings for so long; yet you must remember that it is not merely the religious legend which is preserved but also the rite, the conditioning and the effect that it produces. The religion may change, the race may change, the language may change, but the cause and effect remain, and it is this which tends to keep the legend unchanged.

As Christianity came in witchcraft had to be concealed. Under the Saxons it continued in out-of-the-way communities, or was driven to Wales, Cornwall and Brittany. Many of the cult members, together with remnants of the earlier inhabitants, would live in places to which the conquering race did not go. After a few generations of scanty food a naturally small race, probably intermarrying with Picts and pygmy tribes, would become even smaller in comparison with the big well-fed Saxons, so they became the "Little People", the Pixies—a word surely derived from Picts. This wild race—hunters who had to practise concealment, known to practise some sort of magic rites, using poisoned arrows—would naturally become rather hated and dreaded. A well-known verse describes the situation:

> Up the rocky mountain,
> Down the mossy glen,
> We dare not go a-hunting
> For fear of little men.

They were uncanny people, but though they disliked others trespassing on their domains, they could be good friends if you were kind to them and would help you in time of need. In the Isle of Man there is the Fairies' Bridge which no "South-sider" ever passes without saluting the fairies. This comes from the time when the North side was a separate kingdom often at war with the South. Once the Northerners suddenly invaded the South, driving the Southerners back; the latter were making a last desperate stand at this bridge, when suddenly clouds of long reed arrows, tipped with flints, smeared with some black substance, came at the invaders' rear. The Northerners recognized them; a scratch from them meant death. The cry was raised: "Fly, the little men are attacking us!" and the invaders fled. This was later made into a fairy story to amuse children, or because of people's love of the marvellous; but doubtless it did happen.

In Borneo about fifty years ago I saw the terror raised by a similar flight of arrows from blowpipes. They were about the size and length of thin knitting needles. A scratch caused paralysis in about thirty seconds; death followed in a few minutes. I never ran so fast before or after; but I couldn't catch up with the others of the party.

CHAPTER III

THE WITCH BELIEFS

The after death realm of refreshment before rebirth—full text of the Myth of the Goddess—parallels with other beliefs—the charge read before initiation into the witch community—witchcraft is not anti-Christian—leadership by women rather than men.

EXACTLY what the present-day witch believes I find it hard to say. I know one who goes to church at times, though she is, at best, only an occasional conformist. She firmly believes in reincarnation, as many Christians do. How she or they reconcile it with the Church's teaching I do not know. But, to begin with, the belief in many different heavens, each with their different god, is not unusual. The cult god is thought of as the god of the next world, or of death and resurrection, or of reincarnation, the comforter, the consoler. After life you go gladly to his realms for rest and refreshment becoming young and strong, waiting for the time to be reborn on earth again, and you pray to him to send back the spirits of your beloved dead to rejoice with you at your festivals.

That they believe something of this sort is clear from the myth of the goddess which forms the central part of one of their rituals. It is a sort of primitive Spiritualism.

Witches have no books on theology, so it is difficult for me to discover all they actually believe. With all the thousands of books there are on Christianity I find it difficult to define Christian beliefs. Transubstantiation, for instance. On the other hand, it is easy to give the central idea or myth, which I believe is defined as being a story which affects people's actions. Strictly speaking, in this sense the Myth of Christianity lies in the Crucifixion and Resurrection, and few Christians differ about this. The Myth of Witchcraft seems to be the story of the goddess here quoted. I am forbidden to give her name, so I will call her G.

THE WITCH BELIEFS 41

The Myth of the Goddess

Now G. had never loved, but she would solve all mysteries, even the mystery of Death, and so she journeyed to the nether lands. The guardians of the portals challenged her. "Strip off thy garments, lay aside thy jewels, for nought may ye bring with you into this our land." So she laid down her garments and her jewels and was bound as are all who enter the realms of Death, the mighty one.[1]

Such was her beauty that Death himself knelt and kissed her feet, saying: "Blessed be thy feet that have brought thee in these ways. Abide with me, but let me place my cold hand on thy heart." And she replied: "I love thee not. Why doest thou cause all things that I love and take delight in to fade and die?" "Lady," replied Death, " 'tis age and fate, against which I am helpless. Age causes all things to wither; but when men die at the end of time, I give them rest and peace and strength so that they may return. But you, you are lovely. Return not; abide with me." But she answered: "I love thee not." Then said Death: "As you receive not my hand on your heart, you must receive Death's scourge." "It is fate, better so," she said, and she knelt. Death scourged her and she cried: "I know the pangs of love." And Death said: "Blessed be," and gave her the fivefold kiss, saying: "Thus only may you attain to joy and knowledge."

And he taught her all the mysteries, and they loved and were one; and he taught her all the magics. For there are three great events in the life of man—love, death and resurrection in the new body—and magic controls them all. To fulfil love you must return again at the same time and place as the loved ones, and you must remember and love her or him again. But to be reborn you must die and be ready for a new body; to die you must be born; without love you may not be born, and this is all the magic."

This myth upon which its members base their actions is the central idea of the cult. Perhaps it was coined to explain ideas and rituals already conceived, and to explain why the wiser, older and more powerful god should give his power over magic to the goddess. It is very easy to say this is only the story of Istar descending into hell, but the point of the story is different. Again you can say it is simply Siva, the god of Death and Resurrection; but here again the story is different. It is quite

[1] *See* Note 2 (page 159).

possible that the stories of Istar and Siva have influenced the myth, but I think that its origin is most likely Celtic. In Celtic legends the Lords of the Underworld did prepare you for rebirth, and many living people are said to have entered their regions, formed alliances with them and returned safely, but it needed great courage; only a hero or a demigod dared to risk it. Celtic mysteries assuredly contained rituals of death and resurrection, and possibly visits to the underworld with a safe return. I think St. Patrick's Purgatory in Lough Derg was a Christianized version of this legend.

Primitive man dreaded the idea of being reborn in another tribe, among strangers, so he prayed and performed rites to ensure being born again at the same time and the same place as his beloved ones, who would know and love him again in the new life. The goddess of the witch cult is obviously the Great Mother, the giver of life, incarnate love. She rules spring, pleasure, feasting and all the delights. She was identified at a later time with other goddesses, and has a special affinity with the moon.

Before an initiation a charge is read beginning: *Listen to the words of the Great Mother, who of old was also called among men Artemis, Astarte, Dione, Melusine, Aphrodite and many other names. At mine altars the youth of Lacedaemon made due sacrifice. Once in the month, and better it be when the moon is full, meet in some secret place and adore me, who am queen of all the magics. . . .*

For I am a gracious goddess, I give joy on earth, certainty, not faith, while in life; and upon death, peace unutterable, rest and the ecstasy of the goddess. Nor do I demand aught in sacrifice. . . .

The charge I think came from the time when Romans or strangers came in; it explains a little which would not be known to all in the old days, and identifies the goddess with goddesses of other lands. I think a similar charge was a feature of the ancient mysteries.

I am forbidden to give any more; but if you accept her rule you are promised various benefits and admitted into the circle, introduced to the Mighty Dead and to the cult members.

There is also a small "frightening", an "ordeal" and an "oath"; you are shown certain things and receive some instruction. It is all very simple and direct.

*   *   *   *   *

Among the most common charges against witches is that they denied or repudiated the Christian religion. All I can say is, I and my friends have never seen or heard of such denial or repudiation. My opinion is that in the early days everyone was of the old faith and regularly worshipped the old gods before they were initiated. To people like the Romans and Romano-Britons it would only be worshipping their own gods who had become identified with Celtic ones, so there would be nothing to repudiate.

Possibly during the persecution times if unknown people turned up at a big religious meeting they would be questioned to see if they were spies and might be asked to deny Christianity, as a sort of test. They would never initiate anyone, take him into the circle, unless they knew him well as one of the old faith. When the persecution grew fierce, the cult dived underground and practically only children, born and bred into the cult, were ever initiated. I can well believe that sometimes, if someone not of the blood wished to come in, he might be questioned; but it is as much use to ask the average postulant to deny Christianity as to make him deny a belief in Fidlers Green, which old sailors used to tell about: the paradise where old sailors went, which lay at the far side of Hell.

So I think it possible that though there may have been cases of people denying Christianity, these were very few. To say it is "proof" because many witches were tortured until they admitted repudiating Christianity is like saying that similar testimony is proof that they flew through the air on broomsticks. My great trouble in discovering what their beliefs were is that they have forgotten practically all about their god; all I can get is from the rites and prayers addressed to him.

The witches do not know the origin of their cult. My own theory is, as I said before, that it is a Stone Age cult of the matriarchal times, when woman was the chief; at a later time man's god became dominant, but the woman's cult, because of the magical secrets, continued as a distinct order. The chief priest of the man's god would at times come to their meetings and take the chief place; when he was absent, the chief priestess was his deputy.

In this connection it should be noted that there are certain rites where a man must be the leader, but if a man of requisite rank is not available, a chief priestess belts a sword on and is thought of as a man for the occasion. But although woman can on occasion take man's place, man can never take woman's place. This may derive from the time of the associations of Druidesses of whom the Romans spoke as witches. Whether these were true Druidesses I do not know. It seems to have been a separate religious organization, possibly under the rule of the chief Druid, much in the same way that there was a priest or someone who might turn up at a witches' meeting and be acknowledged chief who came to be called "The Devil" in mediaeval times. I think the use of the witches' circle, in magic, may have come from the Druid, or rather the pre-Druid, people, who built Stonehenge and Avebury and who made use of it to concentrate the powers generated. It is a direct descendant of the circles used in the prehistoric cave magic, though of course it may have come from the East. The Romans suppressed the Druids in the areas they effectively occupied, but I think it possible that a women's section may have carried on even there, perhaps in secret; or maybe they were tolerated and some Romans and Greeks who belonged to the various mysteries, particularly that of Mithras, finding similar organizations, became members, so the goddesses became identified with their classical goddess; hence the wording of the charge.

CHAPTER IV

WITCH PRACTICES

In the past witches were the "bright young things" of the intelligent classes —after the persecution the meetings became small and private—reasons for thinking the cult is very old—the witch rituals—Aleister Crowley, Rudyard Kipling, Hargrave Jennings, Barrat of the Magus and Sir Francis Dashwood—the author's opinion that witchcraft comes directly from the Stone Age, somewhat influenced by classical mysteries—not invented by the Devil—the God of Death as the great protector— Dr. Faustus and the idea of selling one's soul—the planting of information against victims—Manx hatred of informers—instructions in witch writings (given in full)—why witches slept under torture—the use of anointing oils—arrangements for Sabats—the use of oiled bodies—is witchcraft superstition or religion?

THE people who were attracted to the witch cult were chiefly of the intelligent classes comprising craftsmen, soldiers, merchants, doctors, sailors, farmers and clerks. They were all people who wanted adventure, the "bright young things" of the period, combined, of course, with those who always flock to anything secret or odd or religious in the hope of relief; that is, people who are to some degree sexually unbalanced. Then, of course, there was the village wise-woman with her cures and curses, and the inmates of the castles and great houses. Not by any means did all these people "belong", as the witches phrase it—they speak merely of "belonging", never adding to what—but these were the classes of folk who chiefly attended the sabbats of the men of the heaths; and some of them at least were initiated into the mysteries.

The persecution was first directed against the heathens, then against the pagans, and then it turned to their associates in the larger towns and villages. They were a fairly easy mark because they were mostly people who were better off than their neighbours, eating better food and living more reasonable lives. If they got drunk and beat their wives, they were free from suspicion. Anyone who led what we should call a reasonable life and was rather intelligent was suspect and the old cry was: "Kill them all; the Lord will know His own." But the trouble in killing off all the more intelligent people was the loss to the community. So the massacre was stopped in the end; but most of the members of the cult were then dead and only a few were left to carry on. These were chiefly the associates who had been initiated.

Instead of the great sabbats with perhaps a thousand or more attendants it became a small meeting in private houses, probably a dozen or so according to the size of the room. The numbers being few, they were no longer able to gain power, to rise to the hyperaesthetic state by means of hundreds of wild dancers shrieking wildly, and they had to use other secret methods to induce this state. This came easily to the descendants of the men of the heath, but not to the people of non-Celtic race. Some knowledge and power had survived, as many of the families had intermarried, and in time their powers grew, and in out-of-the-way places the cult survived. The fact that they were happy gave them a reason to struggle on. It is from these people that the surviving witch families probably descend. They know that their fathers and grandfathers belonged, and had spoken to them of meetings about the time of Waterloo, when it was then an old cult, thought to exist from all time. Though the persecution had died down from want of fuel, they realized that their only chance to be left alone was to remain unknown and this is as true today as it was five hundred years ago.

The great question which people ask is: "How do you know the cult is old?" This would be easier to answer if I were permitted to print the rites in full. But I am familiar with most forms of ritual including Kabbalistic magic, and they all have certain things in common and work by calling up a spirit or intelligence and commanding it to do their will. All the members stand in a circle for protection and are warned that if they leave the circle before the spirit is dismissed they may be blasted. This is sometimes varied by working in a graveyard and attempting to raise a corpse to get information from it. There is another school which believes that all magical ceremonies should consist of an act together with a rhyming spell. That is, you must show the Powers what to do, then bind them with a rhyme.

Now if anyone in the last two hundred years had tried to make up a rite they would have used one of these methods or something resembling them. The English witches' method is entirely different. They believe the power is within themselves and exudes from their bodies. It would be dissipated were it not for the circle cast, as previously remarked, to keep the power in, and not, as magicians usually use it, to keep the spirits out. A witch can and does move freely in and out of the circle when she wishes.

The only man I can think of who could have invented the rites was the late Aleister Crowley. When I met him he was most interested to hear that I was a member, and said he had been inside when he was very young, but would not say whether he had rewritten anything or not. But the witch practices are entirely different in method from any kind of magic he wrote about, and he described very many kinds. There are indeed certain expressions and certain words used which smack of Crowley; possibly he borrowed things from the cult writings, or more likely someone may have borrowed expressions from him. The only other man I can think of who could have done it is Kipling; but the cult writings are so alien to his ideas and expressions that I am sure he had nothing to do with writing them, though I fancy from some of his works that he knew something about them. There is much evidence that in its present form the rites were worked long before Kipling and Crowley were born. The people who certainly would have had the knowledge and ability to invent them were the people who formed the Order of the Golden Dawn about seventy years ago, but knowing their aims and objects I think it is about the last thing they would have done. Hargrave Jennings might have had a hand in them, but his writings are so involved that I hardly think he could have devised anything so simple and clear-cut. Grandfathers and grandmothers have told folk still living of meetings they attended about a hundred and thirty years ago, when the cult was thought to have existed from all time. Barrat of the Magus, *circa* 1800, would have had the ability to invent or resurrect the cult. But he was mainly interested in ritual magic, which I think would have shown in the rituals. Sir Francis Dashwood, of Hell Fire Club fame, is another who might have had a hand in such a thing, but he was a freethinking diabolist and was the last man to start or invent a new religion; if he did, it would have been something on either diabolical or classical lines. Nor do I think it could have been invented when England was governed by the C.A.B.A.L. (the government of Clifford, Arlington, Buckingham, Ashley, and Lauderdale), and learned men were all Kabbalists; if they believed and worked on Kabbalistic lines they were unlikely to have invented this. It is quite possible that the main parts of the cult might have been brought over from Italy about the time of the Renaissance or even later; but if they were, it would have been as a fully developed witch cult, which was then joined on to the local covens.

I fancy that certain practices, such as the use of the circle to keep the power in, were local inventions, derived from the use of the Druid or pre-Druid circle. At one time I believed the whole cult was directly descended from the Northern European culture of the Stone Age, uninfluenced by anything else; but I now think that it was influenced by the Greek and Roman mysteries which originally may have come from Egypt. But while it is fascinating to consider the cult existing in direct descent from ancient Egypt, we must take into account the other possibilities.

There is, of course, the orthodox Roman Catholic view that the cult was either invented by the Devil or made up by people who hated the Catholic Church. If this was the case, I think it would certainly have shown in the rites or the teaching; but these all run as if the practisers had never heard of either, which points to its being at least pre-Christian. Other people say: "It was a protest against the tyranny of the nobles and the Church." If it were merely that, surely, again, it would show in the rites or the teaching? High taxation may have induced large numbers of people to join the cult in the hope of protection—and this reminds me of the story to the effect that the Cornish people were good heathens, but they were "agin" the Catholic Church. "When they heard of Protestantism they held a large meeting to decide which would annoy the Church more, to stay heathen or to turn Protestant. They decided after much argument that as the Church didn't much mind their being heathens they would turn Protestant." I can very well imagine that perhaps in King John's time, when all England was under interdict—when, as the immortal Smith Minor said, "the Pope made a law that no one might be born, get married or die, for the space of ten years"—then many moderately good Christians, deprived of religious consolation, might easily have turned to the rival religion. After all, the witches' paradise is very attractive to the ordinary man. Similar causes on the Continent may have brought numerous converts to the cult and these may have brought in new ideas. Possibly the Great God, the Protector, the giver of rest and peace, slowly came to be thought of only in his function as god of death and so became more or less identified with the Devil. It is difficult to know exactly what happened; but I believe it unlikely that a large influx of common people in the twelfth, thirteenth and fourteenth centuries would greatly alter the beliefs.

The Church had never taken much notice of sorcery as it was not a rival in the way that witchcraft was, and many Popes and prominent Churchmen were said to practise it. With the Renaissance the spirit of enquiry led to freethinking, and this in turn led to a revival of mathematical magic, astrology, and the Kabbala, to classical studies and thence to knowledge of the classic gods. The legend of Faust was seized upon and the story circulated that to practise magic one had to sell one's soul to the Devil. The best-known treatment of the theme in English literature is, of course, the "atheist" Marlowe's *Doctor Faustus,* whilst a long series of histories and plays on the theme in Europe culminated in Goethe's magnificent *Faust.* It was a credulous age and the story was readily believed: no one seems to have considered whether anyone would think it worth while to suffer millions of years of torture for the sake of a few years' pleasure. There are examples of the existence of such pacts, but it is presumed that either they were based on false evidence planted to convict some poor wretch, or on the acts of stout freethinkers or madmen. Bishop Wilson reports a Manx case in his notebook dated Peel, November 29, 1720, as follows:

"John Curlitt of Murlough, in the county of Down in the parish of Killough, did give himself body and soul to Satan the Devil, who is called Lucifer, after the term of nine years, on condition that he would give him as much money during that time as he should please, on performance of which he did bind himself to the performance of this bargain and promises to fight under his banner during ye said term, which if he do desert he leaveth himself to Satan's pleasure, and promises at the end of

nine years to go himself. Signed with blood, sealed and delivered
to the Devil. John Curlitt."

John Curlitt stoutly denied writing this, saying that it had
been planted on him. The Bishop said it was in his handwriting
and evidently believed in it but, curiously enough, seems not
to have taken any legal action. This may have been a case of
forgery by some enemy, or possibly done for bravado, as there
were several Hell Fire Clubs then in existence. But at that time
the idea of making pacts with the Devil was firmly believed in
and jurists accepted the idea that if anyone were so evil as to sell
his soul for money or any other reason, then it was clear proof
of heresy. And heresy meant death. Seemingly they did not
bother to think that if they executed the criminal the Devil
would get his soul all the sooner.

The Church took measures to obtain information on all
subjects, and to counteract all practices it disapproved of. As the
Manx way may be novel to many, I take the following from *The
Dungeon of St. Germains* by David Crain:

"The summoner annually arranged for the swearing-in of his
Parish Churchwardens and also impanelled the chapter guest,
who, with the wardens, met every three or four weeks under the
chairmanship of the Vicar or Rector. They were bound by oath
to report and present persons alleged to have been guilty of a
breach of the Canon Law. Thus every parish had its body of
nine or ten men, the Skeet, whose duty it was to spy on their
neighbours. In practice the efficiency of the system was bound
to be affected by the restraints governing the conduct of individuals in a small community, and as time went on, the quest men
were increasingly reluctant to perform their office. But even if
they hesitated to destroy the goodwill of their neighbours by
excessive zeal during their year of office, they had a great respect
for oaths, and the result was that the quest exerted a steady
pressure on the life of the Parish, encouraging resentment,
suspicion and fear."

Hence the modern Manx hatred of the informer. By these
means the Church got to know the type of people who were
likely to be witches. The quest men pried and searched everywhere, and they would be the people who searched the belongings
of John Curlitt and found, or pretended to find, the pact with

Satan. They doubtless caused the killing of nearly all the remaining witches and many others, some of whom were not of the cult, until there remained only those who were of families too high to meddle with and possibly some of those who were too poor to be worth looting. Witches would become good Church members to avoid persecution; after all, they had Biblical authority for bowing the head to Rimmon, and it is possible some of these repudiated Christianity at their initiation.

The new terror brought great changes, and, as you could only trust your own children or near relations, the cult became practically a family secret society cut off from all other covens. They held the rites indoors; much had to be curtailed because of the lack of members and many of the rites were forgotten. It was probably about this time that the practice of witches keeping records became common as the regular priesthood no longer existed and the rites were only occasionally performed.

In all the witch writings there is this warning, usually on the first page:

Keep a book in your own hand of write. Let brothers and sisters copy what they will but never let this book out of your hand, and never keep the writings of another, for if it be found in their hand of write they will be taken and tortured. Each should guard his own writings and destroy them whenever danger threatens. Learn as much as you may by heart and when danger is past rewrite your book. For this reason if any die, destroy their book if they have not been able to do so, for if it be found, 'tis clear proof against them. "Ye may not be a witch alone," so all their friends be in danger of the torture, so destroy everything unnecessary. If your book be found on you, it is clear proof against you; you may be tortured.

Keep all thoughts of the cult from your mind. Say you had bad dreams, that a devil caused you to write this without your knowledge. Think to yourself, "I know nothing; I remember nothing; I have forgotten all." Drive this into your mind. If the torture be too great to bear, say: "I will confess. I cannot bear this torment. What do you want me to say? Tell me and I will say it." If they try to make you tell of the Brotherhood, do not, but if they try to make you speak of impossibilities, such as flying through the air, consorting with the Devil, sacrificing children or eating man's flesh, say: "I had evil dreams, I was not myself, I was crazed."

Not all magistrates are bad. If there be an excuse they may show mercy. If you have confessed aught, deny it afterwards; say you babbled under the torture, you knew not what you did or said. If you be condemned, fear not, the Brotherhood is powerful, they may help you to escape if you are steadfast. If you betray aught—THERE IS NO HELP FOR YOU IN THIS LIFE, OR IN THAT WHICH IS TO COME. *If you go steadfast to the pyre,* DRUGS WILL REACH YOU *and you will feel naught, but will go to death and what lies beyond, the Ecstasy of the Goddess.*

The same with the working tools. Let them be as ordinary things that anyone may have in their homes. Let the Pentacles be of wax that they may be melted or broken at once. Have no sword unless your rank allows you one. Have no names or signs on anything, write the names and signs on in ink before consecrating them and wash it off immediately after. Never boast, never threaten, never say you wish ill to anyone. If any speak of the craft, say: "Speak not to me of such, it frightens me, 'tis evil luck to speak of it."

This tells a great deal. It may date from the time of the fierce persecutions on the Continent, and may have then been roughly translated into English. The trouble in dealing with these documents is the witch law: everyone must copy what they will from another, but no old writings may be kept. As everyone is apt to alter things slightly, modernizing the language and making other changes, it is impossible to fix the date when it became current. Clearly it was not written in England. Though bishops may have burnt witches at times, hanging was the only legal death sentence here. It might have been written in Scotland, but Scots would have worded it more clearly I think. It shows one thing: that the craft was powerful. They could bribe jailers to smuggle drugs in to the poor wretches. This I think explains the Inquisition complaints that witches would go to sleep even when on the rack. It must also date from a time when people were becoming literate. Witch-burning on the Continent was by a sort of lynch law; bishops did what they liked, saying that the Church was above the law of the land.

*   *   *   *   *

People still ask me questions about witches because they have heard so many tales about them. Do they go to the sabbat? Is it true they use flying ointment? Why do witches anoint themselves? Did they fly through the air to their meetings on broomsticks? In the old days they usually walked, carrying poles or quarterstaffs, which were useful as weapons. They sometimes used them to make sort of pole jumps over obstacles; they were useful in finding one's way and avoiding obstacles in the dark. In the persecution times, at least, they would put them between their legs and ride on them when approaching the meeting place; or if challenged, as a sign that they belonged to the cult. Failure to do this might mean an arrow between their ribs, and this would usually be smeared with something of the hogsblood and hellebore variety. Finally, they rode these poles in the fertility dance; but riding them meant they got some grease and soot on them, and a pole so stained could be used in evidence against them; so they often took a stick or broomstick which might reasonably be dirty, and used this for recognition or for the jumping or fertility dances. If the place of meeting was distant, they rode horses. They never flew on broomsticks. Nowadays like ordinary people they walk or take a bus or whatever is most convenient.

I have never known witches anoint themselves all over, but I have been shown a recipe for an anointing oil. This consisted of vervain, or mint crushed and steeped in olive oil or lard, left overnight, then squeezed through a cloth to remove the leaves. Fresh leaves were then added and the squeezing repeated three or four times until it was strongly scented and ready for use. It is said that if they lived in the country where they would not be seen, they would strip and rub the oil into their skin and go to the sabbat naked. This would keep them warm enough until they reached the dance. At times they would mix soot with the oil so as not to be seen at night. One of the charges against witches was that they went invisible by night, and, it may be noted, vervain was at one time thought to confer invisibility. They have a very powerful scented oil, which nowadays they speak of as anointing oil. This is only used by the ladies, who dab it on their shoulders, behind their ears, etc., much as ordinary perfume. When they are heated with dancing, this gives off very strong fumes, and most certainly produces a very curious effect. What it is made of is kept a great secret; they had to do without it during the war and for some time afterwards, but supplies are coming forward again. They went naked to the meetings because if they were raided they might not have time to dress and so would leave incriminating clothing behind. Another thing was that they found that the soldiers would usually let a naked girl go, but would take a clothed one prisoner. The slippery oiled bodies also made them hard to catch hold of. In winter they managed to get some sheltered place, a cave or a ruin, for their meetings where they could light fires and be warm. They would wear clothes going and coming to and from these places. The local "quest", inquiring into abnormal happenings, could be trusted to stay at home in winter. They also tell me that in most villages the witches arranged that the first and last house was occupied by a member of the cult, and any strange witch, travelling or "on the run", could go where she would be sure of help and protection. In the villages the members of the cult went clothed to this house and were anointed there. The occupiers of the house never attended the sabbat, but as soon as the last witch had left made some excuse to be seen by as many people as possible in the village, so that if it became known that a sabbat had been held in the neighbourhood they themselves would be above suspicion.

There are many yarns of people getting out of windows and even chimneys when there were non-cult members in the house. Most of the people in those days believed in goblins and devils and were afraid of the dark, so that if the witches were a few hundred yards from the village they were safe from prowlers. Of course, the witches did all they could to foster these fears. They were great leg-pullers, for successful leg-pulling often saved their lives; but their warning tales of the dark were not entirely groundless. The men of the heaths always used poisoned arrows.

After I had written this I received a letter dated September 29, 1952, telling me of a meeting held in a wood in the south of England about two months before, in the traditional nude (luckily the weather was warm). They cast the circle with the Athame, did the fertility dances on broomsticks, performed the proper seasonal as well as other rites, and had some of the old dances. The letter also mentioned three indoor meetings in the last few months where everything had been done very satisfactorily and spells performed which worked! What interests me is the fact that numbers of people meet every year and perform

witch rites because they believe in them. A critic has suggested
to me: "These people are not witches; they only do witch rites
because it gives them pleasure and because they are superstitious."
If that is to be the touchstone, is not a superstition a belief? Is
a Christian who believes in his religion, and also obtains pleasure
and comfort from performing its religious rites, not therefore a
Christian? It is also said, with what truth I do not know, that the
Wee Frees only believe in religions that make you miserable.
Neither the witches nor myself see eye to eye with the Wee
Frees in this respect.

CHAPTER V

THE LITTLE PEOPLE

Pigmy races in Europe and elsewhere—magical power and poison—"fairy"
mistresses and the kidnapping of infants and brides—the "fairy" wife
of the MacLeod clan and the fairy flag of Dunvegan—the Picts of
Orkney and Harold Haarfaga—attendant dwarfs in chieftains' families—
did the dwarfs called Kerions build the megaliths?—Fairies employed at
a battle 1598—intermarriage with non-fairy folk and the small stature
of Manxmen: have they the characteristics of the pixie peoples?

I BELIEVE in the Little People who used to live in the Isle of
Man; but they were not really fairies. There were many races of
pygmies in Europe. They were much the same as the present-day
pygmies of Africa, small people bullied by their bigger neighbours
and driven out of the best lands into the hills and woods and
other inaccessible places. They raid cultivated fields and play
pranks, but if their thefts are forgiven and food is sometimes left
out for them, they will, in return, leave gifts of their hunting
spoils, meat, ivory and skins. It is said that at times they steal
babies and leave one of their own in return, as British fairies
were said to do. Pygmies now live in the same way in Central
Africa, Malaya, New Guinea, the Deccan, Ceylon and the
Philippines. I have known many of them and they all use poisoned
arrows, and are thought to possess magical powers.

There is evidence for these pygmy races in Europe. Many
rock dwellings are too small for a modern man but are very
comfortable for children. People of the invading races who
had driven them out of the best lands were inclined to dislike
them as they raided their crops and killed their cattle. In time
they found that if the Little People were well treated they would
become friendly and help them, as when the Little Folk came to
the aid of the Southerners in their battle at Fairy Bridge. In the
Western Isles of Scotland, as in the Isle of Man, if people had the
Cearrd Chomuinn (Association Craft), a species of handicraft
fellowship, they could get the fairies to come and help them with
ploughing and reaping in return for gifts, as a European in
Malaya gets help from the local Little People, the Saki and Jakoon.

The Fairy Mistress was a recognized type called the *Leannan Sidhe*. She was good and beautiful, but dangerous, and you must not beat her or she would run back to her people taking her children and her dowry of fairy cattle with her. Usually she exacted a promise not to tell of her fairy origin; therefore she must have been of such a size as to be taken for a mortal. Women sometimes had fairy husbands, but they usually had to keep it a secret, or sometimes it was just the fact that he was a fairy that was kept secret, which also tends to show his size. In Scotland the Fairy Mistress often helped her husband with his craft; she could foretell his future, when he would die, or whom he would marry after her death or after she left him; but while the association lasted she was usually very jealous. Fairy Mistresses were said to steal babies and probably they did so to make the race grow stronger. Beautiful girls were regularly kidnapped as brides for the Fairy King, and male fairies often persuaded girls to leave home, as the Highlanders in Scotland used to supply themselves with girls from the Lowlands three hundred years ago by eloping with them or kidnapping them.

The Clan of MacLeods of the Isles was founded by Leod, son of Olaf the Black, King of Man, who was son of Harold Hardraga, the Norse King who was killed at the battle of Stamford Bridge, 1066. His great-grandson, the fourth chief, had a fairy wife, who gave him the celebrated fairy flag of Dunvegan, about 1380. These are all historical people and the flag still exists. This fairy wife was obviously a woman of the small race, who was nevertheless large enough to have a number of children, whose descendants are alive now.

The Little People's homes are often described as conical hills. In Eire the *sidhe* are conceived as living in hills or burial-mounds to the present day. A door, often concealed, opened on the hillside; there were long dark passages leading into many chambers which were sometimes lighted by lamps or torches. Practically all the stories speak of the dark, or twilight. Two miles from Castletown in the Isle of Man a village was excavated in 1943 of a Celtic or, probably, pre-Celtic people. The largest of the houses was a timber-built round-house with a roof like an inverted saucer, made with sods and supported by thousands of oak posts set in graduated rings. The innermost ring formed a room about 18 feet in diameter with a large stone hearth in the centre. This house, about 6,000 square feet in area and 90 feet in diameter, was presumably the chief's or king's house, and he and his family lived in the centre section; all the outer circles were cattle stalls. It is thought to have been still occupied in Christian times.

The house was lit only by the central smoke-hole, which at best could give a sort of twilight. It is certain that at times they would have a watchman on the roof of this house, which would look exactly like a conical hill, and as it is almost as certain that this watchman would go up by a ladder and out by this smoke-hole instead of going all the way to the door and climbing all the way up the hill again, others would also be likely to go out this way. Visitors of the larger races might note this, to them, curious habit of going in and out by the smoke-hole, and it is possible that a confused memory of this led to the story that witches had a habit of leaving and returning by the chimney.

These people were probably members of the numerous races who inhabited Europe in pre-Celtic times, possibly now represented by the Finns and Laplanders, small and very strong as they are described in the folk tales of many people. In the Western Isles there are many Pict houses, conical in shape and made of stone, but when covered with turf they would appear as hills. Beside the well-known Maeshow of Orkney, at Taransay on Harris there is a small one with a guard cell in the entrance passage where the sentry squatted. This cell is built of stone and is two feet five inches high and three feet wide; evidently the sentry was of the Little People! Most of the stone-built passages are only four feet six inches high and some are as long as seventy feet. One can understand that defence needs made a small doorway desirable, also to keep out the cold, but it is unlikely that there was any special advantage in building a long passage where it would be necessary to walk in a bent position; it therefore seems that the average height of the users must have been under four and a half feet. The Norse Bishop of Orkney, writing at Kirkwall in 1443, says: "When Harold Haarfaga conquered the Orkneys in the ninth century the inhabitants were of two nations, the *Papae* (Irish Catholics) and the *Peti* (Picts or Pehts), and he exterminated them both." He goes on to say: "These

Picts of Orkney were only a little exceeding pygmies in stature and worked wonderfully in the construction of their cities evening and morning, but at midday they hid themselves in little underground houses, fearing light" (Horum alteri scilicet peti parvo superantes pigmeos statura in structuris urbium vespere et mane mira operantes, meridie vero cunctis viribus prorsus destituti in subterraneis domunculis pro timore latuerent).

By Highland tradition every chief's family had attendant dwarfs who were thought of as uncanny or fairy folk. They were nearly naked, hairy, and of immense strength; they were mighty archers and were mischievous, fond of dancing and music and able to work magic. They usually did all the work at night. English literature, too, refers to them; Milton's "lubber fiend" nightly churns the cream, and this and other tasks are sung about in Shakespeare's *Midsummer Night's Dream*. In later times perhaps stories of pet monkeys became mixed up with these legends and the whole was made into fairy stories. Sir Walter Scott refers to the aboriginal or servile clans, and describes them as "half naked, stunted in growth and miserable in aspect". They include the MacCouls, Fian's alleged descendants, who were a kind of Gibeonites or hereditary servants to the Stewarts of Appin. Irish manuscripts of the eleventh century state that in the ninth century when the Danes overran Ireland there was nothing in the various secret places belonging to the Fians, or Fairies, which they did not discover and steal. In Brittany legend says that the old people who built the Megaliths were a dwarf people known as the Kerions, small in stature but very strong. There is an expression used "as strong as a Kerion", much the same as one the Scots use in speaking of the Picts: "Verra sma' but unco' strong."

All these peoples seem to be remembered by the same characteristics: good friends but dangerous enemies, very strong, able to disappear at will, having great festivals at night and making use of poisoned arrows. They were persecuted or banished by the Church, which charged them with performing indecent rites and dances. Witches consorted with them and they often intermarried and became the fairy kin in later legends. Scottish witch trials seem to think of witches and fairies as being the same people. As we have seen, they were thought to be experts in magic. Though small they were exceedingly agile and had a great ability for work. They would work at night and be finished by daylight, so they were seldom seen for long, and unless they took service with a man they made off into their mounds at the slightest human interference. Until Victorian prudery covered them with airy gauze they were naked or clad in skin-tight garments. This latter may have been a misunderstanding of the Picts' practice of painting themselves with woad and lime, which makes the famous Lincoln green, the recognized fairy colour. As they were described as being of the same country at the same time, it seems likely that the descriptions of dwarfs, fairies and witches are different people's ideas of the same folk.

There are many cases of nobles employing the Little People. Before the battle of Tri-Gruinard, fought at Islay, Scotland, in the year A.D. 1598, Sir James Macdonald engaged a little man called Du-Sith (Black Elf) who was generally believed to be a fairy. During the action he killed the opposing leader, Sir Lachlan Mor Maclean, with an arrow which was afterwards found to be an Elf-bolt or stone-headed fairy arrow. This disorganized his clan, and the Macdonalds were victors.

Presumably he was one of the Little People, a mighty archer, and his arrow was poisoned, though Sir James may not have known this.

But the belief in a fairy arrow that always killed and a poisoned arrow that always killed is really much the same thing, and he probably thought of poison as being magical; the fact remains, he employed this ally and so gained the victory, and this is a matter of history.

Unfortunately the conquerors, such as Harold Haarfaga, exterminated most of them and reduced the others to a servile state living on the heaths as "heathens", or else they intermarried with their conquerors and merged into the general population. This increased their size somewhat, and when persecuted their descendants denied being fairies or "heathens" and would point to their size to back them up, saying: "Fairies are small, but we are big." At this time it might mean the Bishop's prison with mutilation or burning if one admitted being a "heathen" or fairy. Later the free living ones were exterminated and the town-dwellers disappeared in the general population. I think I can often recognize some of their descendants to this day, short and stocky with very wide shoulders and very strong.

About two hundred years ago the French believed we bred a special race in England to be sailors. They were said to be extremely strong, with very wide shoulders and were all well under five feet high so that they could work under the extremely low decks of British warships. The French are not a race of giants, so there must have been some reason for this belief. A large number of Manxmen did distinguished service in the Navy at this time, and it was said that the Manx regiments (Fencibles) covered more ground on parade than any other British regiment, on account of the remarkable width of their shoulders.

CHAPTER VI

HOW THE LITTLE PEOPLE BECAME WITCHES AND CONCERNING THE KNIGHTS TEMPLAR

Possible return of the Romanized Britons to the goddesses of the Little People—the Normans partly heathens left heathen people alone—alliance between Normans and aborigines—witch cults in France and Normandy—nobles attend the Sabat—exaltation of women by chivalry may connect with the cult of the Goddess—magical ways with animals—the heath people begin to dress in green—Robin Hood and his coven and high priestess—the nature of May Games—the Maypole "a stinking idol"—persecution begun by Popes, extermination of the heath peoples—Christianity wins with "salvation on the cheap"—Lady Glamis and the Duchess of Gloucester suffer—the case against the Knights Templar—the occult rule which they broke—the Templars condition their bodies like the witches and worship a head, use nudity and meet at night—nine official charges against the Templars—the nature of the journey to the Grail Castle—mystery of the disappearance of 14,200 Templars—plunder the main motive of the persecution—the peculiar significance of wearing a cord—Templar rules of secrecy and probability of an "inner circle"—the cult of a death's head links Templars with witches—Templar independence of Bishops and confessors—trampling and spitting on the Cross—the "Templar Hallow" was the Chalice—what was the Holy Grail?—five forms—did it come from a "place between the worlds"?—the Grail as a stone—the legend of the beating of the Cross, revealed 1307—links with the Celtic cauldron—Grail processions and the adoration of heads—kissing the feet of a skull—the High Priestess's ritual position—the Templars may have joined in wild cults after return from the East.

IN ENGLAND these Little People were mostly pre-Celtic aborigines, but among them would be many Roman-Britons who had stayed on after the Saxon conquest. Most of these would be Christians, but all their priests had fled. At that time many of the people of Rome thought that all her troubles arose because they had deserted the old gods. Presumably the Roman-Britons might think the same; but the priests of the recognized Roman faiths had been abolished two hundred years before when Rome turned Christian. The Little People had goddesses who were identified with Diana and Aphrodite, so it would be only natural for Romans who wished to worship their own old gods, who had no temples, to call on and worship these.

This influx might have brought about some changes in the cult, but the main objects would I think be unaltered. What they wanted was prosperity and fertility for the tribe, a life after death in happy conditions, and reincarnation into their tribe or nation.

Slowly these people came to be on speaking and trading terms with the Saxons, probably combining together against the various Viking invasions. Then Christianity came back again. The kings and townspeople accepted it, but the country people, the pagans (*pagani*—people dwelling in the country), the villagers, the heathens (the "people of the heaths"), were mainly of the old faith, which is why we use those two names to describe non-Christians to this day.

Next came the Norman invasion. The Normans were heathen Norsemen who had received large grants of land from the French king on condition that they became Christians and did him homage. We might well call them rice-Christians nowadays. They are said to have had a sect in Rouen, their chief city, which worshipped Aphrodite; this was, it appears, only suppressed in the twelfth century. William the Conqueror's father was Robert the Devil and he was credited with witchcraft. William's son, William Rufus, was also said to be a witch leader. The Normans were few among a very large population of Saxons whom they had reduced to serfdom. These were good farmers and workers, living in places where the lord could reach them. Being so handy they were forced to work the land for the lord of the manor and pay taxes. The heathens, the people who lived in the wilds, were few and inaccessible, and it was difficult to force them to pay taxes or give any feudal dues and so they managed to live more or less independently. They were thought of by the people from towns as uncanny folk addicted to magic.

The Saxons hated their conquerors and were sullen and rebellious. It is more than likely that the heathens were at first rather pleased to see their Saxon conquerors so discomforted and were quite willing at times to enter into relations with the Normans, giving service as hunters and possibly as miners, in return for exemption from all taxation. These relations would most likely take place when the Norman manorial lord already belonged to some cult of the same nature in France.

That there were such cults is proved by manuscripts of the

Church Coureans in France which tell how the ladies of the nobility used to ride to the nocturnal revelries or sabbats of Bensozia, the Diana of the ancient Gauls, also called Nocticula, Herodias and the Moon. They inscribed their names in a register and after the ceremony believed themselves to be fairies. Here we have the fact that the nobles were in friendship with people who held some form of witches' sabbat, and the people who celebrated these ceremonies were apparently thought of as being both witches and fairies at the same time. It is notable that the goddess was, like the witch-goddess, known by many names and identified with the moon. Of course these liaisons were only formed by the more free-thinking or less priest-ridden people. Edward the Confessor would not have joined them, but William the Conqueror or William Rufus might easily have done so. In connection with these rides to Bensozia I may mention a story which the witches tell me, that in the olden days they used sometimes to go to big meetings at a distance on horseback, dressed in queer clothes, looking like spirits, shouting and singing to frighten people. Can some such rides have started the legend of the wild hunt? Possibly the legend gave them the idea. It should be noted that the historical Raymond de Lusignon married a fairy named Melusina from whom the Lusignon kings of Jerusalem and Cyprus were descended, and Melusina is one of the names of the witches' goddess. At this time, though the people of the heaths would attend the religious ceremonies, only the priests and priestesses would be initiated, passing the tests and taking the oaths. That is, anyone well affected to the people and the cult could attend these ceremonies. This would account for the stories of masked people who would come riding to attend the sabbat. They were known to be nobles, keeping to themselves and taking no part in the proceedings but dancing and feasting among themselves. It was also well known that at times six thousand people were present at one sabbat.

It may or may not be a coincidence, but the idea of chivalry arose about that time. In an age when women were treated as drudges, and Churchmen seriously debated whether they had souls or not, the lesser nobles, that is, the class of people who were apt to attend the sabbats, suddenly evolved a code of deference to women. It amounted to placing certain gracious ladies on pedestals and treating them with the greatest possible respect. At first it seems it was only to those ladies who would "play the game", so to speak; but in time it led to the mending of manners towards the whole sex. Had this a connection with the cult of the goddess?

The Normans took some of the men of the heath into their service as grooms, hunters and other menials, when their knowledge of animals became useful. I think they had some extraordinary knowledge and love of animals which in later times descended to the Horse Whisperers in Ireland, who, according to reliable stories, could tame the most savage horse by simply whispering to it. In my youth in Scotland there was a sort of mystical secret society known as the Horseman's Word among farm servants. The members of the society were supposed to have dealings with the Devil, and they certainly did have an uncanny power over horses. I believe the Kirk and the Trade Unions combined crushed them, though they may still exist in secret. The secret taught in this society or cult was that men and animals were brothers, of the same stock, and should be thought of and treated as brothers. I think something like this was believed and practised by the Horse Whisperers, and accounts for some of the things they were able to do, and that something like this lay behind the stories of witches' familiars. It all came from the practices of the people of the heaths, and this in turn from the ancient peoples who first attempted to influence animals by magic. This, however, is simply my theory; I cannot give any proof of it. As the country opened up, the races may have inter-married and the men of the heaths would tend to grow larger. A mixed breed is always better physically, but by intermarrying they would tend to lose those queer hypernormal powers which seem to occur when there is much inbreeding. These are most common with identical twins and less common with ordinary twins, but undoubtedly other people possess them also. They are apt to be hereditary, but the witches have formulae for producing this form of auto-intoxication, of escape into the world of faery. It cannot be induced, however, if people are unsympathetic, as many Saxons were, to these powers, which they thought devilish.

The Little People were vivid, emotional, thriftless; the Saxons were stolid, hardworking, religious and respectable. The fact that the hated lords had dealings with the Little People and attended their shocking meetings did not tend to heal the breach. The wilder and less religious of the lords would ride great distances to attend a sabbat. The witches have stories of people stealing out of houses at night to attend, borrowing their masters' horses; or maybe the master himself saddled his own horse and rode off to the meeting without telling his wife. These worn-out horses back in their stables by cockcrow may have given rise to stories of pixies riding the horses. In the Castletown Museum is a stable-door key with a holed stone tied to it to stop the fairies from riding the horses. These Roman-British fairy girls were often very beautiful and many of the men attending the sabbat brought back fairy wives and usually had very happy marriages. This was quite common among small farmers who lived in isolated places; but it was frowned on by the more respectable part of the community.

Times slowly changed. The lords were no longer Normans. Many had married Saxons, some had legitimate or illegitimate children by Roman-British women, and the race had become English. The people of the heaths were no longer half-naked savages clad in skins; they wore clothes dyed with woad treated with lime, which, as I said before, produced the famous Lincoln green—a most excellent camouflage enabling the Little People to vanish by diving into the bushes. The Robin Hood story was spread, the tale of the wonderful archer who never missed his aim. Robin was a common French-English name for a spirit and Hood was a frequent variant for Wood, and has further been derived from the Scandinavian Hod, a wind god, variant of Woden. Robin Hood, therefore, though he probably had a historical existence also, was a mythical form into which a witch-leader could easily transform. He had his coven of twelve, including the High Priestess, Maid Marian, all dressed in Lincoln green. It was perhaps rather more respectable to go to a foresters' than to a witches' party. The bright young things among the Saxons went and strolling friars turned up. Gradually these parties evolved into the May Games.

It must be realized that the old-time public May Games were much more, very much more, than a few school-children dancing round a maypole. They were often what people now call "orgies". For instance, the Judge, who together with the Jurats ruled Alderney in the Channel Islands until recently, told me that until the year 1900 the old customs were kept up to such an extent that any unmarried Alderney woman could say to any eligible Alderney man within the year: "You were with me at the May Games, the child in my body is yours, you must marry me," and he was forced to do so.

But nowadays there is only one such old custom still in force. Any Alderney person who has a bottle of rum with him on May Day may take milk from anyone's cow to make rum and milk, and the owner may not object. But even that custom is dying out because of the price of rum.

The Puritan writer, Philip Stubbes, speaks of the maypole as "a stinking idol, of which it is the perfect pattern, or rather the thing itself", meaning that it was phallic. He also says: "Both men and women, old and young, . . . go to the woods and groves, where they spend all the night in pleasant pastimes and in the morning they return. I have heard it credibly reported, viva voce, by men of great gravity and reputation, that of the maids going to the woods overnight, there have scarcely the third part returned home again undefiled."

Even allowing for Puritan exaggeration it would seem that the Witches' Sabbat was nothing more than the ordinary pastimes of the people, any excesses being deliberately exaggerated by their opponents.

If things had been let alone some of the more startling practices would have ceased, or have been performed only in private. But in 1318, and again in 1320, Pope John XXII issued ferocious Bulls against witchcraft pronouncing it to be heresy. In the resulting persecution, which continued for centuries, the people of the heaths were practically exterminated. There were no more big sabbats, as the organization was crushed and the surviving members were either in the households of nobles or among the secret cult members.

The early trials show us what happened. People said: "We are good Christians; we have always done these things so as to reap a good harvest." In many cases it was the parish priest who had led the fertility rites, and the people said they had not been told it was wrong; in fact the priest said it was right. At first only penances and fines were imposed, but as the Church grew stronger torture and fire were used. The old religion made one great mistake. It had stated that paradise was reserved for the initiates; that the ordinary folk when they died went to a kind of spiritualist heaven, a happy hunting-ground: but it was one where they had to work, as only initiates could obtain the required learning which took them to a paradise where they were rested and refreshed, till they were ready to be reincarnated on earth again.

Christianity at first promised what has been irreverently called "salvation on the cheap". "Abjure your heathen gods, believe in the three gods who are one, and you go straight to a glorious heaven, where you are a king with a golden crown, never working but playing harps and making wassail for ever." All who refused this offer would burn in Hell. There is an old story of a Scots minister who preached: "And, dear brethren, after Judgment Day I will stand on the battlements of heaven by the richt han' o' the Lord, and we will luk down on ye a-writhing in the awfu' fiers o' Hell. And ye shall scream in agony: 'O Lord, Lord, we didna ken.' And the Lord will luk doun on ye wi' His infinite goodness and mercy, and He will say unto ye: 'Weel, ye ken the noo.'"

We laugh today, but it was not a joke when people believed that it would happen. The heathens had no hell with which to scare people; they simply stated that the best heaven and the best reincarnation were for the rich and clever. While the respectable, hardworking folk of the towns disliked the men of the heaths and were shocked at their doings, the lesser nobles were not ashamed of their contact with the magic of witches or sorcerers, as they did not consider it a serious offence, and several Popes have been said to have practised it. The Gospel of St. John begins: "In the beginning was the Word," and it was thought that by knowledge of that word of power King Solomon had made the spirits work for him. Manuscripts were sold at high prices, giving the rites and words of power used by him and professing to teach others to do the same.

The lesser gentry who made no secret of their practices were easy prey and yielded much loot to the Church, until the persecution turned to higher game such as Lady Alice Kyteler in Ireland. Lady Glamis, who I believe was an ancestor of the Queen, was burned alive in 1537 as a witch! The Duchess of Gloucester was condemned to the dreaded Bishop's Prison in Peel Castle, Isle of Man, where she languished sixteen years until her death. Her companion Margery, the Witch of Eye, was burned alive and Roger Witche (note the name) or Bolingbrook, a clerk and churchman, was drawn from the Tower of London to Tyburn and there hanged, beheaded and quartered.

There is also the celebrated case of the Knights Templar. They were attacked suddenly and their destruction by fire and torture brought enormous amounts of loot into the hands of State and Church. There have been innumerable books stating the cases for and against this order, so this may be of interest. The witches tell me: "The law always has been that power must be passed from man to woman or from woman to man, the only exception being when a mother initiates her daughter or a father his son, because they are part of themselves." (The reason is that great love is apt to occur between people who go through the rites together.) They go on to say: "The Templars broke this age-old rule and passed the power from man to man: this led to sin and in so doing it brought about their downfall." If this story was not merely invented to explain the fall of the Order, it would seem that the Templars may have known and used some of the old magic. Is it possible that the heads or skulls they were said to worship may simply have been images representing Death and what lies beyond?

The main ground for this theory is that the witches think they recognize indications that the Templars conditioned their bodies in the way they themselves do to produce magic; how they do so, however, I am forbidden to mention. But they also say that one of the charges made against the Templars at the Grand Process in Paris in 1316 was "that at their reception into the order they denied Christ, declaring he was not God but a man, and that they had no hope of salvation through him and that they did not believe in the sacraments of the Church". Though they do not deny Christ or the sacraments, witches generally do not believe in them, which was at least "unusual" at that date. At her initiation a witch is always received into the circle with a kiss on the mouth. Templars received a similar kiss. But both were tortured to make them say it was elsewhere. Another charge was that the Templars worshipped a head, variously described as having sometimes three faces, sometimes simply a human skull or death's-head: that they believed that this head had the power to make them rich, cause the trees to flourish and the earth to become fruitful. (We would call it a fertility cult.) At initiations Templar candidates were stripped nearly or entirely naked; they held their meetings and initiations secretly and by night, as witches do.

My books of reference give the official charges made against the Templars as follows:

1. Denial of Christ and the defiling of the Cross.
2. The adoration of an idol.
3. A perverted form of the Mass.
4. Ritual murders.
5. The wearing of a cord of heretical significance.
6. The ritual (or obscene) kiss.
7. Alteration in the words of the Mass and an unorthodox form of Absolution.
8. Treachery to other sections of the Christian Army in Palestine.
9. Immorality.

With regard to No. 8, no body of men fought so bravely and so long in Palestine, so this seems to be only a trumped-up charge.

With regard to Nos. 3 and 7, if this were true it must have been done by the Templar priests, and not by the fighting Knights, but only Knights were tried. No action was taken against any Templar priest.

With regard to No. 9, all the Crusaders and the ordinary clergy were charged with this at some time or other. There seems little evidence that the Templars were worse than the others.

But with regard to 1, 2, 5 and possibly 4 and 6, I think there may have been some base for the charges. The idol was said to be called Baphomet. Some writers say this is a corruption of Mahomet; but in those days the Crusaders surely knew Mahomet was a man and a prophet, and not an idol. It was also said to mean Bapho Metis, the Baptism of Wisdom, with no explanation given of what this wisdom consisted. Another story was that it was coined from the first letters of the following sentence written backwards: *TEMpli Omnium Hominum Pacis*

*A*Bbas: the Father of the Temple of Universal Peace among men. Now could this word have been coined to represent *the Consoler, the Comforter, the giver of Peace, Death and What Lies Beyond*?

Many writers say that the journey to the Grail Castle really depicted the journey of the soul through the Underworld to reach Paradise, and that this is made very clear by various exhibitions which are given to the Hero whenever he cannot understand certain incidents. (See the *High History of the Holy Grail*; also J. S. M. Ward, *The Hung Society*, for full details.) Now this secret castle was said to be in a far land and to belong to the Templars. To reach it you had to undergo trials or to ask certain questions, know certain secrets and secret words (passwords); in other words, "initiation" into a more or less secret society whose secrets were a magical talisman, which had five forms, or five things which were different but the same; a secret of prosperity and fertility, and a secret of resurrection or regeneration connected with a lance which dripped blood into a cup or cauldron.

All this might be taken to be equivalent to saying that it was possible for man to attain a happy after-life without the aid of the Church, or that you had no need to worship Christ in order to obtain salvation. This is exactly what the Church charged the Templars with believing. As this struck right at the heart of the Church's teaching, the Church said that all those who held these views must be destroyed; hence the various trials and executions.

I do not think it has ever been explained exactly what happened to the bulk of the Templars. Records show that about eight hundred were executed or died under torture; but this was out of fifteen thousand Knights scattered all over Europe. There were also about twenty-five thousand priests and serving brothers, who do not seem ever to have been persecuted. So seemingly about forty thousand people dived underground and disappeared, as the witches did later. One curious point about this persecution is that the Templar priests were never charged. If there is any truth in charges 3 and 7, it could only be the work of the priests. It was said they addressed the thief on the cross, which would probably have meant Barabbas—surely an unlikely person to turn into a god. Another story was that they called Christ a thief because He claimed to be the Son of God when he was the Son of Man. If they had said the liar or the pretender on the cross it would have made sense.

Actually, I think there is no doubt that it was a case of "here are wealthy people whom we can loot", and advantage was taken of the fact that some of these Knights were suspected of being followers of an old religion. However, a number of false charges were brought at the same time, firstly because of a misunderstanding of the import of some rites, but mainly because, if the real truth were known, much public opinion would have been in their favour.

Charges are made at times because of a misunderstanding of certain ceremonies, etc. For instance, the Romans accused the early Christians of being cannibals, because it was said that at their meetings they ate the body and drank the blood of their God! And during the First World War the Turkish police raided the English Church at Jerusalem, tore up the altar and dug up all the floor, because they had heard that the priest in charge had recently made two canons at the altar—canon had only one meaning for them.

Wearing a cord of heretical significance. To modern writers on the Templars this has always seemed a curiously pointless charge at a time when all monks wore such a cord or girdle. But though the Inquisitors may have been scoundrels, they were certainly not fools. The way they stressed this charge shows that their object was to discredit the Templars with the general public in a way that would cause them to forget their great services to Christendom. So it is obvious that this cord or girdle was thought to be unorthodox at least. *The Chronicle of St. Denis* states very emphatically: "In these girdles was their mahommerie." It has been said that this meant that they were secretly Mohammedans; but to charge them with embracing Mohammedanism would have been the most damning charge, and it was never even hinted at. In those times, a Mammot was used to denote a doll or an idol and Mahommerie would mean "having to do with idols". They were said to have used these cords to bind the skull or head which they worshipped. To a witch this binding of a skull could have a meaning. That the Templars attached some meaning to these cords seems clear. In the *Chronicle of Cyprus* we hear that a Templar's servant removed (? stole) his master's girdle. When the Templar discovered this he immediately killed the servant with his sword. Again, an outsider is said to have heard a knight instructing some novices, telling them to guard these cords well, wearing them concealed beneath their clothing, as through them they might attain great prosperity.

Now all this might apply to the consecrated cord which witches possess and use in many ways. All those I have seen are coloured, usually red, though I have known other colours used. They value them as they do all their working tools and naturally would be most annoyed if anyone removed (stole) any of them.

It might be noted that about this time the Churches accused witches of "Raising Storms, Human Sacrifice and Wearing Girdles". A curious combination!

I am forbidden to tell of the uses a witch makes of her cord, and I doubt whether the Church knew, or they might have mentioned it at the trials. Or perhaps they did know and did not wish this knowledge to be made public.

All this may be the merest coincidence, and I only give it to show what some witches now believe. For myself I see nothing impossible in it. It is not suggested that the Templars were members of the witch cult, simply that some of them may have had memories of an old cult of Death and Resurrection, and while more or less Christian still had leanings towards it, and possibly practised some of the magic connected with it.

It must be remembered that novices were forbidden to speak of anything which occurred at their initiations, *even to another member*. If they were only forbidden to tell anything to outsiders, it might be simply that, like Freemasons and others, they had secret Rites of Initiation; but novices being forbidden to compare notes points, it would seem, towards certain parts of the ceremony not being given to all novices, or, alternatively, that different explanations were given of the same ceremony. Possibly certain commanders favoured the old gods and might introduce certain practices, and the fact that in many cases novices said they were threatened with swords to make them go through the ceremony would point to this. Or there may have been an Inner Circle in the Order, who picked out certain novices as likely members who could work magic: in other words, people who had slight mediumistic powers. These might not necessarily be attracted to the Old Faith, and so needed a certain "frightening" to make them do certain acts, such as spitting on the Cross.

Having done this, the novice might feel he was an outcast, and so be more amenable to obey the orders of the Inner Circle. This theory would explain that seemingly the greater number of the Knights knew nothing of this practice, nor had seen the head or skull, but had heard that others had seen it elsewhere. Or it is conceivably possible that during a very long ceremony certain things were done which would not be noticed if the novice's attention were not drawn to it. If the Grand Master stood for a minute or two with his arms crossed on his breast, who would notice it? But if you were told that in that position he represented the god of "Death and What Lies Beyond", through whom you would gain salvation, you would take notice, and taking that notice might be taken by the Church as thinking they had no hope of salvation through Christ, or rather, that it was possible to obtain a happy after-life and regeneration without His aid.

If you were shown a head or death's head later, told it represented the same god and to do reverence to it, that might be termed adoration of an idol by the Church. If another novice were shown the same skull and told it was simply an emblem of mortality or the head of a saint, the most orthodox churchman could not object.

There is some evidence that these skulls existed. Some were found, one in Paris.

There is a curious Templar story of a skull that brought good luck or fertility. A noble lady of Maraclea was loved by a Templar, a Lord of Sidon; but she died and was buried. Such was the force of the knight's love that he dug up her body and violated it. When a voice told him to return in nine months' time he did so and found a *skull on the leg bones of a skeleton* (a skull and crossbones). The same voice told him to "guard it well, for it was the giver of all good things". It became his protecting genius, and he defeated all his enemies and gained great wealth. Later it became the property of the Order. And through it the Order gained its great wealth and power. Writers say that this would seem to be a garbled account of a ceremony of Death and Resurrection, perhaps seen by some outsider.

There are many ancient legends of such heads or skulls: that of Bran the Blessed in the Mabinogion, the Bleeding Head in the Story of Peredur, and others, all bringers of victory and prosperity, reminiscent of the old legends of Adonis and Astarte, and of Horus who was begotten by the dead Osiris.

The Templars may have attempted practices which, while sheer heresy to a witch, were founded on her methods. Witches teach that to work magic you must start with a couple, a male and a female intelligence being necessary, and they must be in sympathy with each other; and they find that in practice they become fond of each other. Sometimes it is undesirable that they should fall in love. Witches have methods by which they try to prevent this, but they are not always successful. For this reason, they say, the goddess has strictly forbidden a man to be initiated by or to work with a man, or a woman to be initiated by or to work with a woman, the only exceptions being that a father may initiate his son and a mother her daughter, as said above; and the curse of the goddess may be on any who break this law. They think that the Templars broke this law and worked magic, man with man, without knowing the way to prevent love; so they sinned, and the curse of the goddess came upon them.

To my own knowledge, using these witch methods is very apt to cause a fondness which could lead to an "affair" if it were not suppressed from the start. But that means doing two things at once, trying to produce sympathy and at the same time killing all natural fondness, and it is much easier to do one thing at a time. In wartime Templars may have gone all out for the one thing, not knowing of, or not caring for, the consequences.

The Templars had many peculiar privileges. They had their own priests, who were entirely independent of the local Bishop, being answerable to the Pope alone. Templars confessed their sins to each other and were given absolution, being scourged meanwhile; this meant that no mention of any unorthodox teaching would get outside. There is no reason to say that from the beginning the Templars were unorthodox; it may have just happened that owing to peculiar circumstances this Order was organized in a way that meant that secret doctrines could be taught safely at a time when free thought was strongly suppressed. I should imagine that most of the Templar Priests knew what the rites meant; why, for instance, the novices were stripped of all or nearly all clothing.

The number three played a very important part in the lives of the Knights. For example, the Ritual Kiss and the symbolic denial of the Cross were said to occur three times in the ceremonies. There are many other cases of the use of the numbers three, five and eight that occur in Templar usages which suggest that these numbers had a special meaning for them.

The most curious of the charges against the Templars, and one which seems to have some foundation, was that of trampling or spitting on the Cross and the denial of Christ. Its import seems to have been little understood by the Knights, and it would seem that different explanations were given to different people. Petrus Picardi told the Inquisitors that it was a test of fidelity, and had he been brave enough to refuse to do as he was told he would have been sent at once to the Holy Land; but this also proves that he and others were threatened with death if they did not do it. Gouarilla, Preceptor of Poitou and Acquitaine, said the denial was in imitation of St. Peter's having denied Christ thrice. Other excuses were given for spitting or trampling on the Cross.

Sometimes this cross was said to be a Crucifix, at others a cross cut or painted on the floor, which again would point to one man's being initiated in one way and the rite being performed differently for another. But in all cases it seems to have been a severe test of obedience on the part of the novice, as time and again we read that other Knights had to threaten him with drawn swords before he would do it, and that he only did it to save his life.

Charge No. 4 seems to point to novices actually being killed who refused to conform, though this point does not seem clearly proved.

The shape of the Templar churches, circular outside, octagonal within, is peculiar to them. It is said to be copied from the Mosque of the Dome in Jerusalem, which they thought was the Temple of Solomon, and it is possible that this may have influenced them; but the Templars, of all the Crusaders, had more intercourse with the inhabitants of Palestine; they should very soon have learnt when and by whom that mosque was built; that is, by Omar, the mosque always being known as the Mosque of Omar. So it appears to me that these churches were built for some special ritual purpose, and that purpose involved working in a circle. It may be noted the Grand Master of the Templars always carried a Wand of Office, crowned with an octagon. I have never heard any suggestion as to its meaning.

I suggest that the rites performed may at times have included circumvallation round a central point or altar, that it included a dramatic form of Death and Resurrection or regeneration, or a visit to the underworld, and a pact or alliance with the god of Death and What Lies Beyond, and that the *point within the centre of the circle* may have had a great meaning for them. Also that the number eight had some significance. It is said that this is simply because the Templar cross had eight points; but could it not be that they revered the number eight and therefore gave their cross its eight points?

Another great Templar "hallow" was the Chalice, the Cup. As I have said, the witch also reveres the Cup, which seems to date back to the old fertility cults. It is a curious fact that the Church disliked and discouraged the story of the Holy Grail, though they could not entirely prevent its being popular as a "romance". The original versions appeared about 1175 to 1225; then the source of supply seems to have been cut off. Can it be that the Church brought pressure to bear? Henceforth writers simply made rehashes of the old materials, adding stories of King Arthur and his knights, etc.

Now the Grail is a sort of hallow or talisman. It brings fertility to the land and it feeds its worshippers. It has many forms, but it is always a fertility- and a food-providing object. It seems to have had five forms:

1. A reliquary.
2. The platter or cup used at the Last Supper.
3. A jar or bottle in which St. Joseph received the Blood from the Wounds of Christ.
4. A Sacred or Talismanic Stone.
5. The Chalice of the Eucharist.

In all these cases however it seems to have no material substance, but to have come from a sort of fourth dimension, to which it returned swiftly again. Shall we say it came from and returned to that place *between the Worlds*, or something like the Witches' Circle?

We are told the Grail is a mystery which must not be revealed to the uninitiated. *The High History of the Holy Grail* says that the Grail appeared *in five several manners that none ought not to tell, for the secret things of the Sacrament ought none to tell openly but he unto whom*

God hath given it. Does not this point to there being an inner meaning to the Grail story, that the meaning of the sacred object varied, according to the understanding of the initiate, or shall we say that different explanations of the meanings of an object were given in higher grades of initiation, and that the outermost explanation was the Chalice, but that in all there was the "feeding" and fertility implication?

There are indications that the Church knew of or suspected some secret rite among the Templars and that it was of a phallic nature, for with fiendish cruelty they attached heavy weights to that organ when torturing the unfortunate Knights, as if to say: your rites centre round that member, so we torture you there to extract the most damning evidence. The men of the fourteenth century quite understood the principle of "making the punishment fit the crime".

In *Parzival*, by Walfram von Esehenbach, the Grail is a stone which is under the protection of a body of Knights Templars who are chosen by the Stone itself. On the Stone appear written the names of these guardians when they are yet children (does this not point to novices being initiated into a cult while still children, as in the witch cult?). So also the Stone chooses a wife for the King, whom alone he is allowed to marry (Priestess of the Cult?). This Stone brings food to its worshippers. In the Diu Crone Version Gawain achieves the quest, asks a long-awaited question and thereby restores to life the *dead* King Guardian. Is this not a regeneration or reincarnation motive?

The *High History* also says:

"After this came two priests to the cross, and the first ordered Sir Pereeval to withdraw from the cross"; and when he had done so, "the priest kneeleth before the cross and adoreth it, and boweth down and kisseth it more than a score of times and manifesteth the most joy in the world. And the other priest cometh after and bringeth a great rod and setteth the first priest aside by force, and *beateth the cross* with the rod in every part and weepeth right passing sore. Pereeval beholdeth him with great wonderment, and sayeth to him, 'Sir, herein seem you to be no priest. Wherefore do you do so great a shame?' 'Sir,' sayeth the priest, 'it nought concerneth you of whatsoever we may do, nor nought shall you know thereof for us.' Had he not been a priest,

Pereeval would have been right wroth with him, but he had no will to do him any hurt. Therewithall he departed. . . ."[1] Later the King Hermit explains that both priests loved Christ equally, and that he who beat the cross did so because it had been the instrument of bitter pain and anguish to Our Lord. Can this explanation have been inserted to explain and justify a ceremony of kissing and beating, or of defiling the cross, such as it was alleged that the Templars performed? The *High History* was written about 1220; it seems to show that the then ceremony was old and had a legitimate explanation in the eyes of those who took part in it. The writer was probably a Templar priest or someone who knew and approved of their practices, and possibly wished to explain away any rumours which had been spread.

It has occurred to me the witches have a rite which involves kissing and then beating an object, with the intention of charging it with power. It is not a cross and they do not speak or think of it as a cross; but on reading this account it struck me that an observer at a little distance might easily mistake it for one. It is rather cross-shaped. If the Templars used the old magic, they would be most likely to perform this rite, and rumours might spread about.

The alleged Templar rite of defiling the cross only became known to the world during the persecution and trial of 1307, ninety years after the *High History* was written. There are many traces of a fertility cult in the Grail stories. The "Hallows" themselves seem to be connected with such cults.

The Grail, the Cup or Chalice, is like the Celtic Cauldron. It restored the dead, and brought fertility back to the land. The King, in the *Mabinogion*, gives Gawain a sword which each day drops blood. There is a head and spear which drops blood in connection with a cauldron of fertility in the adventure of Peredur, vaguely said to be connected with the murder of a relation of Peredur by witches at Glaucesier. A sword or dagger dropping blood (or wine) into a cauldron would have great meaning to witches, and they have a head or skull tradition. Could the story be a hidden way of hinting that an ancestor of Peredur had gone through the circle to Death and returned, and so Peredur himself was of the Witch Blood and entitled to know the

[1] Dr. Sebastian Evans, *The High History of the Holy Grail*, pp. 89, 191.

Mystery of the Cauldron? Most scholars agree that the bleeding spear is phallic.

In the *Merlin* MS., Bibliothèque Nationale 337, there is a Grail procession which passes through a wood singing: "Honour and Glory and Power and everlasting joy to the *Destroyer of Death*." Could not that be a chant in praise of the goddess? Or could it be really to disguise a chant: "Honour and Glory and Power and everlasting joy to the *destroyer of the fear of Death*"? That is, to the givers of Regeneration, *Death and what lies beyond*.

Jaffet, a knight from the south of France, deposed that at his reception he was shown a head or idol and told: "You must adore this as your saviour and the saviour of the Order of the Temple," and he was made to worship this head by kissing its feet and saying: "Blessed be he who shall save my soul." Cettus, a knight received at Rome, gave a very similar account. A Templar of Florence said he was told: "Adore this head; this head is your god and your Mahomet," and said that he worshipped it by kissing its feet.

There seems to have been no questions asked as to how you can kiss a skull's feet. Can it perhaps be explained by some rite resembling the following witch practice: in the old days it was said that "when the god was not present, he was represented by a skull and crossbones" ("Death and what lies beyond", or "paradise and regeneration"). Nowadays this is symbolized by the High Priestess, standing with her arms crossed to represent the skull and crossbones. The worshipper kisses her feet, saying a sort of prayer beginning, "Blessed be . . ." and the intention following is that indicated by Jaffet and the others, the words not being exactly the same, as it is very unlikely that they would be: probably he spoke in French, which was then translated into monkish Latin and retranslated into English many years afterwards: doubtless the witch-words have also changed. I remember a German witch saying to me on his first introduction to the English rites: "But this is pure poetry!" Now none of it rhymes, but it is beautiful, though very unequal, which I think proves that someone poetically inclined rewrote much in the last two hundred years.

During this prayer to the High Priestess she opens out her arms to the Pentacle position. She then represents the goddess,

GERALD BROSSEAU GARDNER
The author is Director of the Museum of Magic and Witchcraft,
Castletown, Isle of Man

Representation of a magician's circle at the Museum of Magic and Witchcraft, Castletown. The design of the circle is taken from a manuscript of the Clavicula of Solomon the King

Memorial at the Museum of Magic and Witchcraft, Castletown, dedicated to Margrate ine Quane and her young son who were burned alive on the charge of witchcraft at Castletown, A.D. 1617, and to nine million victims in Europe who went to the stake on the same charge

or regeneration, signifying that the prayer is granted. "Thus she has been both god and goddess, male and female, death and regeneration, one might say bisexual." Now in Payne Knight's illustrations of Baphomet, said to be the Templar god, he is shown as both male and female or bisexual; sometimes a skull appears, sometimes the moon. Whether there is really any good proof that these are the Templar gods I cannot say. All this may be mere coincidence.

No. 5 is the accusation of the Templars wearing cords or girdles, with which they used to bind their skull-god. As we have seen, the Church similarly accused witches of wearing cords or girdles which have a ritual meaning for them. For myself, I see nothing impossible in the Templars having used it as a witch does.

The Templars were drawn from the small nobles, the classes who, while good soldiers and at times giving largely to the Church, were often at loggerheads with her; and some at least of these classes had a witch or fairy connection. When Christendom was vanquished by paganism, and the Crusaders, after all their efforts, were thrown out of the Holy Land, there was naturally a period of disheartenment throughout Christendom, a feeling that God and Christ had failed them. Through their long association with the East the Templars may have become more tolerant and more broadminded than their stay-at-home countrymen, and some at least may, on their return to Europe, have been tempted to go among the only people with whom they might talk freely, people with whom they already had associations in their youth, and they may have attempted practices which, while sheer heresy to a witch, were founded on her methods.

I think it may be far-fetched to suggest any connection between the Templars' alleged practice of crossing their legs and the skull and bones, because many tombs of the period show knights with their legs crossed, including some who were not Templars and who were never in the Holy Land. It could, of course, simply mean the cross, but would it not be more reverent to do this with the arms? The god Mithra is very often shown with two attendants with torches, who usually have their legs crossed. This was very much a soldiers' cult, and so might appeal to the Templars and others; but I have not found any other connections.

CHAPTER VII

THE WITCHES AND THE MYSTERIES

Affinities of witches with Voodoo and ancient Mysteries—Macchioro's "The Villa of the Mysteries"—the new birth is the identification of self with the divinity—the Lesser and Greater Mysteries were the centre of Greek life for 1100 years—an account of the Villa and eight stages of the liturgy revealed by the paintings—the inner essence of all Mysteries the same—the wild dances show happiness—doubtful effects in Africa of putting down tribal dances—corruption of the Mysteries by the Romans—mention of mysteries by Plato, Thales and Stoboeus—happiness of the ancient peoples attributable to these cults.

I HAD always believed that witches belonged to an independent Stone Age cult whose rites were a mixture of superstition and reality and had no connection with any other system. But during my short stay in New Orleans, though I did not succeed in getting into Voodoo, I noticed some suspicious resemblances which made me think that Voodoo was not solely African in origin but had been compounded in America out of European witchcraft and African mythology; and when I visited the Villa of the Mysteries at Pompeii I realized the great resemblance to the cult. Apparently these people were using the witches' processes. I know, of course, that ancient and modern writers have agreed that the Greek mysteries of Dionysus, Zeus, Orpheus, Zagreus and Eleusis were similar; therefore since each mystery had different rites and myths but was the same, this must mean that they had some inner secret.

In his learned work *The Villa of the Mysteries*, Professor Vittorio Macchioro has this to say on the subject: "The mystery is a special form of religion which existed amongst all ancient peoples, and among primitive peoples still preserves very considerable importance. Its essence is the mystic *palingenesis*, that is to say, a regeneration brought about by suggestion. In its most perfect stage this *palingenesis* is a veritable substitution of personality: the man is invested with the personality of a god, a hero or an ancestor, repeating and reproducing the gestures and actions attributed to him by tradition."

Only those deities who, owing to their own mythical history, bore within themselves the elements of new birth, Demeter, Dionysus, Isis, Atys and Adonis, could confer *palingenesis*, the identification of the self with the divinity, owing to the special conception which the Greeks had of the relations between life and death. The postulant passed through the divine myth, revived the life of god and passed, together with the god of sorrow, into joy, from life unto death. Professor Macchioro gives this account:

"All the mysteries operated after the same manner. They consisted in a sacred drama and a series of ritual acts, which reproduced the gestures and actions attributed to the Divinity. This is the principle of the Eucharist, the eating of bread and drinking of wine to identify oneself with His acts. It was not an objective but a subjective drama, its essence being the repetition of that which according to tradition had been wrought by God. It was led up to by preliminary instruction, heightened in effect by visions and ecstatic suggestions conducting the initiated, himself an actor in them, to communion with God. The dramas became a veritable event in the life of the man, like the sacrament, transforming him completely and assuring him happiness after death. At first the mystery was a purely magical ceremony, but with time it acquired a spiritual and moral content. The mystery religions had an enormous influence on the Greek conscience, enabling it to comprehend the value of the Christian message.

"Orphism was the most important of these deriving its name from its alleged founder. It was a particular form of that orgiastic and ecstatic religion which originated in the worship of Dionysus and consisted in living over again his myth. Zagreus, the son of Zeus and Korè (Persephone), is slain at Hera's instigation by the Titans who tear him to pieces and devour him except for his heart which Athenē saves and of which is born, as the son of Zeus and Semelē, the second Dionysus. *Palingenesis* here consisted in dying and being reborn again in Zagreus. Mankind had birth from the ashes of the Titans smitten by the thunderbolt of Zeus in punishment for their crime. This is why all men bear the burden of the Titans' crime; but as the Titans devoured Zagreus, man has within him also the nature of Dionysus. Theologians said that it was the Titanic nature innate in the body from which man must free himself to reunite with the Dionysiac nature through the agency of the mysteries. Thus the Orphic Mystery took a lofty moral and spiritual significance and exercised great influence on lofty souls such as Heraclitus, Pindar and Plato, and when Christianity spread it was Orphism that gave the fundamentals to the Pauline theology.

"Orphism soon came in contact with the rural cult at Eleusis whose celebrated mysteries were without ecstatic and orgiastic elements. Contact with Orphism transformed the cult adding the element of redemption; from the fusion were born the Eleusinian Mysteries as known throughout antiquity. These consisted of two parts, the Orphic centring round Zagreus and celebrated at Agrai, a suburb of Athens, and termed 'the Lesser Mysteries', and the Eleusinian centring round Demeter and Korè, celebrated at Eleusis itself and termed 'the Greater Mystery'. The former were the necessary preparation for the latter; they conferred the *palingenesis* in Zagreus, the new life which rendered the initiated worthy to have access to the higher teaching of the great mysteries.

"Protected by the state, glorified by artists and poets, they were the centre of Greek life and flourished uninterruptedly from the eighth century B.C. to the year A.D. 396 when Eleusis was destroyed by mobs of monks. The secrets, protected by law, were respected; we know as little of the Lesser Mysteries as we do of the Greater, that supreme vision which crowned the series of ceremonies on the last day. Scholarship made repeated efforts to discover what took place until the Villa of the Mysteries was discovered. This lies in the Street of Tombs, Pompeii, outside the Stabian Gate, and is divided into two separate parts by a corridor. The north-east part is like an ordinary Pompeian house; the north-west part is arranged peculiarly. The central portion is formed by a large hall decorated with frescoes and is reached from the corridor by passing through two small rooms, entering the hall through a small side door; the way out from the hall is by a large door opening on to a terrace. This large hall was originally a Triclinium (dining room), and the two little rooms were originally Cubiculi (bedrooms); they have all suffered alterations to adapt them for a purpose other than that for which they were intended. The paintings contain the answer, for they extend all round the walls of the hall regardless of angles and apertures. They contain twenty-nine figures, almost life-size, dressed in the style and costume of the Greeks and resembling the Attic paintings of the second half of the fifth century B.C.

"It is evident that we have a single act divided into several episodes depicting the story of one draped female figure who reappears in all the episodes. The story is a series of liturgical ceremonies by means of which the woman is initiated into the Orphic Mystery and attains communion with Zagreus.

"1. The liturgy begins with a maiden who, aided by an attendant and two young boys, one holding a mirror before her, and superintended by a priestess, is performing her bridal toilet. She is draped in the *sindon*, a ritual veil which was placed on the neophytes in the mysteries; she is the mystic bride, the catechumen, preparing to celebrate under the symbol of matrimony her communion with Dionysus. It is she who is the protagonist of the entire liturgy.

"2. Draped in the *sindon* the maiden reverently approaches a nude youth evidenced to be a priest by the high Dionysiac boots he is wearing. This *embades*, under the tender guidance of a priestess, is reading a charge or ritual from a roll in order that the neophyte may be made cognisant of the rules, or maybe of the significance of the initiation.

"3. Thus instructed and enabled now to share in the rite, the maiden, still draped in the *sindon* and now wearing a crown of myrtle, moves to the right bearing on a ritual dish food in slices to take part in a lustral repast. Before a sacrificial table is seated a priestess assisted by two attendants; with her left hand she uncovers a dish brought by one attendant and in her right hand she holds a branch of myrtle on which the other attendant, who has thrust into her girdle a ritual roll, is pouring a libation by means of an *oenochoe*. This is the lustral *agape* which must be celebrated before the communion, as was the custom in primitive Christianity.

"4. After the celebration of the *agape* the neophyte is worthy of a new birth, represented allegorically. A Satyr and Satyra are seated; a fawn is stretching out its muzzle towards the Satyra who is offering it her breast; on the left Old Silenus gazes on the scene playing ecstatically on a lyre. In the myth the child Dionysus was transformed into a kid to hide him from the wrath of Hera. This kid which is being suckled symbolizes the infancy of Dionysus, and Silenus is present because he is to be the pedagogue of the god; the scene represents symbolically the new birth of the neophyte. She is born again in Zagreus under the form of a kid, which is why there is found on the golden tablets buried with the initiated at Sybaris the soul of the dead appearing before Persephone and saying: 'I am born again.'

"5. The neophyte is born again in Zagreus; she has begun to live the life of the god, but terrible tests await her. Silenus seated on a double plinth shows her a hemispherical silver case on which a youth gazes in ecstasy while his companion holds on high behind him a Dionysiac mask. Silenus turns to the neophyte, identified by the *sindon*, and utters that to her which visibly fills her with terror. She shrinks back as though to flee and makes the gesture of one who would banish from her eyes a terrible vision. The hemispherical case at which the youth gazes ecstatically is a magical mirror; he is fascinated and falls victim to a hallucinatory monoideism and, as happens in crystallomancy, sees in the mirror a series of visions which have their centre and starting point in the mask and life of Dionysus. He sees unrolling itself in the mirror the life of the god, sees how he was rent to pieces and devoured by the Titans, and, in short, sees the future destiny of the neophyte, who, if she would be born again as a new creature, must die together with Zagreus. It is this dread Dionysiac death which he announces to the maiden. It is a divination which is being wrought and it is Silenus, first the pedagogue and then the mystagogue of Dionysus, by whom it is wrought. Besides including the annunciation of the future death of the neophyte, this scene includes further repetition of the most important gesture attributed by myth to the god: Dionysus when a child beheld in a magic mirror, fashioned for him by Hephaistos, his future destiny. Another tradition is that the Titans slew Zagreus by showing him in a mirror his own misshapen face, so distracting his attention that they killed him. Now as the sacramental drama consisted in the repetition of the actions of the god to obtain by this imitation communion with him, this explains why the neophyte, or the youth on her behalf, gazes on the mirror as Dionysus did so as to become as Dionysus and die with him.

"6. The neophyte after receiving the annunciation would now become the mystical bride of Dionysus, and to signify symbolically this wedlock she is about to uncover a huge *phallus* which she has brought in a sacred basket. She places this on the ground and seems humbly to crave the assent of a winged semi-nude figure, shod with the Dionysiac boot, a ritual roll in her girdle and a rod in her hand. It is Talatē, the daughter of Dionysus, the personification and executrix of the initiation.

"7. Talatē stays her gesture with her hand and lifts the rod whilst the maiden kneels bewildered and terrified with her face well-nigh hidden in the lap of a compassionate priestess, to endure the ritual flagellation which replaces and symbolizes death. Physically she does not die, but she passes symbolically through death and dies mystically as the stigmatists die crucified in Christ.

"8. Dead with Zagreus, she is now born again with him; that is to say, she has become a bacchante and is no more a woman but a divine human being. We see her now nude and frenziedly dancing, aided by a priestess who holds the *thyrsus*, the symbol of the new Dionysiac life. The spirit of Dionysus has descended upon her. Man has become God, and Dionysus is present unseen at the miracle. We behold him in the space between the fifth and sixth scenes, half reclining in the lap of Korè, one foot unshod according to the rite, contemplating with divine indifference all that man may suffer for him. Thus the mystery is wrought.

"The Orphic Basilica, the great hall, was the hall of initiation or *stibade* and was entered through the small doorway after preparatory sacrifices had been performed in the little rooms adjoining, as proved by fragments of sacrifices found there. After entering the *stibadium* and receiving initiation the neophytes went out through the large door on to the terrace, where one may suppose a banquet took place in festive celebration of the event. This arrangement corresponds to the Orphic *Baccheion* discovered at Athens. To form this private Basilica its makers took advantage of the Triclinium and the two adjacent cubicula, rearranging and adorning them with paintings suited to their new purpose, and it was not without good reason that this Basilica was placed in a suburban villa. The Orphic Mysteries were as we know prohibited by the Senatus Consultum (De Bacchanalibus) after they had given rise to scandals; but the most curious point is that according to Livy these scandals happened precisely in Campania and the initiations were by women and took place by day. Our liturgy shows us the initiation of a woman and the enormous window proves that the initiations were made in the daytime. This Orphic Basilica, in days of old the secret meeting place of the initiated, enables us today to penetrate the secrets of the Greek Mysteries."

More recent investigations have shown that this villa belonged to some of the Imperial family and the high priestess in the frescoes has been identified as a portrait of the owner, though her name has not yet been ascertained. I showed a picture of these frescoes to an English witch, who looked at it very attentively before saying: "So they knew the secret in those days."

All these ancient mysteries had this much in common. They were often the means by which one passed from one class to another; they made a woman marriageable, for instance. Many, however, were connected with a future life, but this was kept secret.

I think all priests in ancient times were regenerated, made holy by some such means, and at times laymen also; whether this made them minor priests or not I do not know. In Athens we know that practically all the Greek population were initiated, including the slaves, and that the State paid the fees of the poor; but no foreigner was ever initiated and the secrets were protected by law, as this was thought to be necessary for the good of the State. We also know that they kept the gods' names a secret.

Christian writers were accustomed to speak of these mysteries as orgies, and Chesterton, speaking of the *Bacchae* of Euripides, says: "Nowadays, imagine the Premier going off with the Archbishop of Canterbury to dance with unknown fair ones on Hampstead Heath." But they did this because the gods wished them to and not for pleasure only, though doubtless they did enjoy it. Nowadays people might be shocked if they thought they enjoyed it, or even if they obtained fresh air and exercise that way, as the Jews were highly shocked at Christ's breaking the Sabbath.

There is a story that Père Lachaise let off King Louis XIV with the slightest penances for cold-blooded massacres and suchlike, which he thought quite natural things to do; but he was most highly shocked and gave a very heavy penance because after some battle Louis ate a mince pie on a Friday, not knowing there was some tiny bit of meat in it.

So when old writers who were initiated say "all the mysteries were the same", surely they must mean the inner essences were the same. A heathen examining the various Christian sects, Catholic, Roman and Orthodox, Presbyterian, Methodist and Church of England Churches, would say they are at heart all the same. They all worship the Triune God, the Father, the Son and the Holy Ghost. Though some may pay more honour to the Virgin and the Saints than others, and the people who thus worship are on the whole good and worthy people and obviously would not so worship if the religion were evil, so when we find that the greatest and best men of the ancient world belonged to the initiates, we may be sure the mysteries were not just orgies. Indeed we know, as shown above, a little of what they were. Lewis Spence in his *Occult Encyclopaedia* says:

"Pictures, mosaics and sculptures show the initiates as naked, one carrying corn, another fire, some sacred baskets with serpents, women, or goddesses, initiating men . . . these were secret cults into which only certain people were admitted after preliminary preparation . . . After this mystic communication or exhortation (the Charge), the revelation of certain holy things, then communion with the deity; but the mysteries seem to centre round the semi-dramatic representation of a mystery play of the life of the god."

I think it is at least plausible to believe that all this was not play-acting, but that there was a serious reason behind it. That they believed that, while the gods wished them well, they were not all-powerful, that they needed man's help; that by performing certain rites men gave them power; also that the gods wished men to be happy and that acts which gave men pleasure also gave the gods joy and power, which they could apply to their own uses as well as to the benefit of man.[1]

The wild dances showed that the gods wished men (including Chesterton's Premier and Archbishop) to be happy, and not to be puritanical. This ecstatic dancing also produced power and visions of the future, some of which at least came true. For this reason these rites were valuable to the State, and were protected by law, so that no foreigner might ever know them. Evidently priests and priestesses who could foretell the future, however dimly, who could calm down the most dangerous politicians and cause them to work for the State instead of striving to disrupt it, were of the greatest value. On the other hand, if the existence of this power were known, the secret might be discovered and used by enemies, both to cause political disruption, a sense of pacifism or surrender to the enemy.[2]

Again I repeat that I do not say that they could in fact do all this; but I do say that witches believe that they themselves can, and I think that people in Athens in high places held similar beliefs. Because people all over the world are apt to do certain things and believe certain things in certain circumstances, and while these beliefs can occur independently, where they are very alike I am inclined to suspect a connection. I expect many people will attack this view and I only hope that they will. Discussion and criticism is the only way to arrive at a satisfactory conclusion.

The first and strongest argument against my views will be, I think, the belief "that to gain power and to stop the people thinking of their miseries, the priests and kings encouraged the greatest excesses". In Africa at present the action of missionaries and the Government in putting down big tribal dances is said to have caused the present political unrest and campaign of murder. And it is certain that the mysteries made the population happy

[1] *See* Note 3 (page 159).
[2] *See* Note 4 (page 159).

and quiet. That at them there were orgies at times is common knowledge; no one attempts to deny the facts; but whether they were much more than beanfeasts is a moot point. Something, usually wine, was drunk, but I believe that by law it was two parts wine and three parts water and you cannot raise much debauchery on that. They danced wildly, and it is just possible that some sort of sacred marriage was performed, but it consisted mostly in long religious services and in long and tiring processions.

These are no secrets to be protected by law, or to prevent foreigners or criminals from seeing or knowing. Nowadays it would be different. The press would concentrate on the spicy bits; the country would ring with it, all sorts of women's unions, county councils and Sabbath-day protection societies would combine, and the whole machinery of the law would be put in motion to prevent it. But in those days no one would have thought anything of it! Anyone could have an orgy in his own home. Anyone was free to open a night-club in his house, to have as many pretty slaves as he pleased to entertain his guests; there were absolutely no inhibitions, the result being that everyone, after sowing a few wild oats, settled down to a quiet married life, having many places handy where he could let off steam if he wanted to. I think it was not because of repressions that all the people joined and it was not to get away from your wife because, if I'm not mistaken, you took your wife and your daughters and your grandmother and your mother-in-law, and they all kept the secret; and this went on for about a thousand years. When the mysteries came to Rome it is true that the local criminals infiltrated into them and there was trouble; these being removed the cult went on happily. Unfortunately the Romans were gross feeders and heavy drinkers, and commonly drank undiluted wine contrary to the usual Mediterranean tradition. But by and large, the mysteries seem to have had a good effect, though not the same as they had in Greece. Probably the reason was that owing to early excesses and the coming of Christianity, the true secrets were communicated to only a very few. At least that is what I think, and I would like comments on this. But in their true state I think the mysteries were really good. Porphyry, Iamblicus, Synesius, all refer to them and their objects and revelations. "Of what the disease of the spirit consists, from what cause it is dulled, how it can be clarified, may be learned from their philosophy. For by the lustrations of the mysteries the soul becomes liberated and passes into a divine condition of being, hence disciplines willingly endured become of far greater utility for purification," says Plato.

He continues: "On entering the interior part of the Temple, unmoved and guarded by the sacred rites, they genuinely receive into their bosoms divine illumination, and divested of their garments they participate of the divine nature." The same method takes place in the speculation of Thales: see Proclus on the theology of Plato, vol. 1, and *Ede anima ae daemona*, Stoboeus, Dr. Warbarton's trans.: "The mind is affected and agitated in death, just as it is in initiation into the mysteries, and word answers to word, as well as thing to thing; for to die, to be initiated, is the same; with hymns, dances and sublime and sacred knowledge, crowned and triumphant they walk the regions of the blessed."

But it was also said: "The rites are not equally good for all; there are many more Thyrsus-bearers than Bacchic souls. Many have the fire indeed, without the power to discover it": that is, "All are not true initiates." "Who can question the extraordinary power of woman over man? Whether questioned or reasoned about, it always remains the irresistible factor of life. This power is a divine gift and therefore induces more than merely sex attraction. With any woman, young, beautiful and vivacious, her influence for good or evil is overwhelming. When moved by high principle and purpose, womankind can elevate and ennoble man."—*A Suggestive Inquiry*, etc., by A. J. Attwood.

Not only in the sacrifices to the generative gods, but in the worship of every god the religious ceremonies of the Greeks and of all the ancient peoples were happy and involved feasting, dancing in the gods' honour and rejoicing generally, with the exception of the later Jews and possibly of the Egyptians: many of the Egyptian festivals were happy but some were not, because they had many and diverse gods. It is highly probable that the early Jewish rites were festive also, though reformers constantly strove to abolish all mention of this, and there is no doubt that the Bible has been tampered with to this end.

CHAPTER VIII

OUT OF THE LAND OF EGYPT?

Pennethorne Hughes's account of the origin of African magic and the trans-
planting of it to the new world as Voodoo—the witch tradition of
coming from the East—witch swords—possible link with Egyptian
worshippers of Set—similar elements in the witch cult and the Mysteries
—the Greek teacher would make man the standard for beliefs, not
adapt man to a code.

In Mr. Pennethorne Hughes's book we have the following
interesting passage on page 23:

"Studies of the magic and ritual of Africa have in the last few
years established with some certainty that all the systems for the
disturbance of consciousness practised by the African negro are
derived from ancient Egypt. Thousands of Africans were trans-
ported to the New World and many of those who went to Haiti
from 1512 onwards were of the finest African stock and perhaps
carried with them a synthesis of the cults then existing in the
Congo. It is easy to show how close the parallels are between the
voodoo they practised and mediaeval witchcraft. The mysteries of
Delphi and Eleusis, or the Roman cults, probably had the same
origin. The ritual of the Druids is said to copy that of Osiris; Odin
himself is believed to be merely a frosty version of Osiris. Witchcraft almost everywhere had two main derivatives to which its
other formative influences became attached; the fertility cults
persisting from the indigenous inhabitants of any area, and the
latter 'magical' practices derived through direct or distorting
channels from the centralizing Egyptian source. Witchcraft as it
emerges into European history and literature represents the old
palaeolithic fertility cult plus the magical idea and various
parodies of contemporary religions."

All this is intensely interesting to the witches themselves.
They have vague stories that the cult comes from the East, the
Summer Land, combined with a story that it had existed since
the goddess went to the Land of Death. Of course they know that
they have been vaguely in touch with various sorcerers and wise

men, and it is said that in the old days when witches were persecuted, the sorcerers were not, and that they secretly used witches
as mediums to attain success in their arts. With the help of these
clairvoyants they became successful as prophets, and probably the
witches took several of their ideas and certainly some of their
tools. I have seen seven witches' swords; of these, four had
apparently been made for sorcerers, according to the pattern
prescribed in the *Key of Solomon*, with Hebrew inscriptions on hilt
and blade. There are two in the museum in Castletown. Other
implements bear Hebrew inscriptions and so seem to be connected with Hebrew or Kabbalistic magic. But stores do not
cater for witches, and a poor witch has to get her tools as
and how she can. There is also a great resemblance to what
are now unimportant parts of Freemasonry; but while the
Masonic working seems to be of little use, or in other words it
does not work, the witch practice is most useful. Everyone who
has witnessed both is convinced that the one is copied from the
other and believes that the witch practice must be the original
working before it was "bowdlerized".

The statement that all the systems for the disturbance of
consciousness used by African negroes are derived from ancient
Egypt is extremely interesting, as is the natural suggestion that
they took these powers with them to America. In ancient times
there was widespread trading up the Nile, across and down to the
Congo. I had always thought of the Africans going in for human
sacrifices and orgies of rum, methods I believe entirely alien to
the Egyptian spirit. I was told in New Orleans that it was not
only negroes who attended the Voodoo festivals but that many
whites went as well. It was well known there that Voodoo
festivals were often held by the lakeside and bodies of police
were regularly sent out to prevent them. But the police, who
were mainly Irish, would search regularly several places where the
festivals were not and then report back that they could find
nothing. They would then go to the meeting, strip off their
uniforms and join in the revelries. This indeed is a common
joke in New Orleans. I noticed several resemblances between
witchcraft and certain Voodoo practices. I was also told that
it had been clearly proved that Voodoo was not African but
was compounded in the French West Indies by French half-

castes, from European magic, inverted Roman Catholicism and mixed memories of different African religions. I cannot say if this is right; but if some of these French half-castes had a witch tradition this would account for all the resemblances. For all over the world when faced with certain problems people are apt to solve them in the same way. If the knowledge now practised in West Africa is derived from ancient Egypt, there is no reason to doubt that some witch practices may have come from the same source to Europe via the Roman and Greek mysteries, which all seem to be derived from ancient Egypt. I feel that the Egyptian cults were too severe and respectable to go in for the blood practices used by Africans. I think Pythagoras, who is generally credited with bringing the mysteries to Greece, was not the sort of man who would have had anything to do with blood sacrifices or other objectionable practices. But it is conceivable that there were two sects, the worshippers of Set, as well as those of Osiris, who crept in with the plea: "There is a short cut; if you cannot work magic properly, you can gain power this way." The writings of witches speak with horror of the practice of sorcerers using blood to gain power. But the evil knowledge may have kept pace with the good and may account for some of the statements against the cult which I am still inclined to think were Christian libels or came from a misunderstanding of the rites.

The mysteries, in Greece and Rome at least, were secret cults to which only the initiated were admitted after being prepared and purified and passing ordeals to prove their worth. They were also given instruction on how to attain to a happy and satisfied life on earth, to know the teachings of the brotherhood within the cult, how to attain reunion with their loved ones who had passed on, how to be reincarnated in this way, and, probably, in ways of persuading the gods to favour them and grant their requests; in other words, magic. Each of the ancient mysteries at Cabrai, Samothrace and Eleusis had a different myth and was dedicated to a different god, Zeus, Dionysus, Orpheus or another, and performed different ceremonies; but since the classical writers say the mysteries were all the same, the teachings behind the myths may well have been identical.

The tribal rites of most primitive peoples include purification, tests of fortitude, instruction in tribal lore, sexual knowledge, charms, religious and magical knowledge, and often a ritual of death and resurrection. Now the witch cult contained most of these things; therefore, as we believe that all the mysteries were basically the same, the Greek mysteries must have taught the same things. Was it not perhaps because in Greece these systems were allowed so much influence and even political power that Greece gave us so much? After all, other small States have also given the world art and learning. From Greece, however, in spite of constant wars and upheavals Eleusis and its teachings made an impression on human thought which is difficult to overestimate or eradicate. As the late Dean Inge said: "What has the religion of the Greeks to teach us that we are in danger of forgetting? In a word, it is the faith that Truth is our friend and that knowledge of Truth is not beyond our reach." William Brend says in *Sacrifice to Attis*: "Modern man is not free; he is bound by his terrors in the directions which most vitally affect him, yet he longs for the freedom of the Greeks. He shows this in the way he strives to hide his fears. Here lies his hope; for, though he neither has freedom nor understands it, it is his ideal. This involves setting up a standard of conduct based upon knowledge and truth and not upon revealed guidance."

It would seem that the Greek priest or teacher would take a man as he was and fit a code to him, instead of torturing him to comply with a predetermined ethic, thus anticipating the work of C. J. Jung, whose method is always to build up from whatever elements of belief he finds in a patient a system of personal myth which becomes a rationale for his conduct. Any lessening of the impulse to impose herd-standards of behaviour has, says Brend, "always met with bitter opposition, and it is not to be lessened by setting out the failure of modern society with its wars, sicknesses, poverty and senseless cruelty, for this irrational opposition is impervious to argument. We see the Roman priest in his temple crudely and literally emasculating his followers. Today the father in the Church, the school and the law court is equally destroying the manhood of his sons by means less rough but none the less effective because they are so widespread."

Representation of a witch's cottage at the Museum of Magic and Witchcraft, Castletown, showing ritual altar

Altar prepared for the initiation of a witch in the Southern English coven, showing, *inter alia*, incense burners, a scourge, wine cup, pentacle, wand, sword, an aspergillum for consecration by water, and the ceremonial book on stand

17th-century portrait of a male witch with his familiar (a cat)

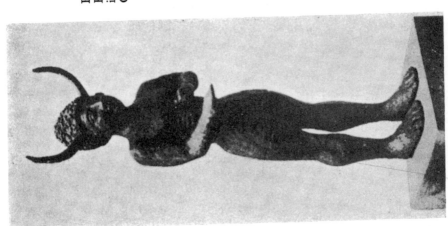

Bronze figure of a Horned God of Death in a ritual attitude, Cyprus *circa* 1500 B.C.

CHAPTER IX

IRISH WITCHCRAFT

The case of Lady Alice Kyteler and the Little Peoples—the case of Dionysia
Baldwyn in Exeter, 1302—indications that the courts of justice believed
no harm in witchcraft—rumours of a cult in South Ireland—copies
of the witch rituals—the charges copied out afresh in each generation
—the essence of magic is to raise power.

THE most famous single case of Irish witchcraft is that of Lady
Alice Kyteler of Kilkenny. The Bishop of Ossory charged her
with witchcraft under the new Bulls issued by Pope John XXII,
and she was tried in 1324. The court obviously believed she had
been practising witchcraft, but saw no particular harm in it.
Though supposed to convict her they let her off as lightly as
possible and discharged her, much to the Bishop's disgust; much
as a Manx court in 1659 found Mrs. Jane Ceasar not guilty of
witchcraft, though the Bishop managed to get her sentenced to
"abjure her witchcraft, the following Sunday in Malew Church"
(a curious case of "not guilty but you must promise not to do it
again".) The lady was forced to abjure in church and spoke
with a play of words which satisfied the court, though the
commentators said: "It would make her accusers very unhappy if
they really believed her to be a witch." As nothing more is recorded
it is to be presumed that the matter was allowed to drop. Later
Church records show that she died and was buried in the ordinary
way; the Ceasars were people of very good position.

But the Bishop of Ossory was of sterner mettle than the
Manx Bishops. Relying on the Pope's Bulls he attacked again,
accusing Lady Alice of denying Christ, having indecent ceremonies with a Robin Artison, or Robin the son of Art, at the
cross-roads, and of a whole list of the usual stock charges,
including having a staff which she anointed with ointment and
galloped through thick and thin—presumably an ordinary
fertility dance. Again he could not obtain a conviction; the
nobles protected her and she got away to England. The Bishop
had to content himself with flogging, torturing and burning her

servants by a sort of ecclesiastical lynch law. Among the charges against her was one of sweeping the dust inwards. In the Isle of Man it is a common superstition that you must sweep inwards or you will sweep the luck away.

In Lady Kyteler's case there was sufficient evidence to prove the existence of witchcraft and of a coven of thirteen. Most likely she was in communication with an Irish branch of the Fairy or Little People who celebrated rites similar to those used in England and to those of Dionysus in ancient Rome. The second charge against her was that "she was wont to offer sacrifices to devils, live animals which she and her company tore limb from limb, and made oblation by scattering them at the crossways to a certain demon called Robin, son of Artes, or Robinartison". As remarked above, the name Robin was a common one for a spirit, this time perhaps an artful or tricky one ("artes"). The action seems like a description of a number of Bacchantes who used to tear animals in pieces in the Dionysian frenzies, since the devouring of an animal victim was supposed to symbolize the incarnation, death and resurrection of the divinity. There was another charge of sacrificing red cocks to Robin, who is described as being "Aethiopia"—in other words, a negro. It would be very unusual to find a negro with an English name in Ireland at that time, so I presume that Robin mixed soot with his protective ointment so as not to be recognized. They were probably members of a local cult who carried out magical ceremonies to bring themselves luck. There were thirteen people accused but Robin was never arrested, so the "tricky spirit" was probably of high rank or a churchman. Thus we may presume that a witch cult which had some resemblance to the cult of Dionysus was in full swing at that date and consisted of both Irish and English members.

Mr. Hughes mentions that the municipal archives of Exeter show that in 1302 the Grand Jury found that "Dionysia Baldwyn does often receive John and Agnes de Wormhille and Joan de Cornwale of Taignmouth who are witches; and the said Dionysia consorts with them." The name Dionysia suggests to me that her parents belonged to some such cult and that the priest who christened her had no objections, though many Church councils had fulminated against cults of Diana and the moon. John,

Agnes and Joan are all witch names, according to Dr. Margaret Murray; Wormhille (Dragon Hill) might be accidental, or it might have some meaning. One would have expected the local Bishop to have secured a conviction; but the court apparently would have none of this and thought: "Why shouldn't witches have a good time or practise their arts?" As in Ireland, they had no objections to Lady Kyteler's "dirty work at the cross-roads".

Actually in those days the courts seem to have believed that there was no harm in witchcraft. There were no particular laws against it. The *Sites Partidas* of Castille, *circa* 1260, says it should be punished if it causes harm, but that it is thought valuable for curing diseases. The Assizes of Jerusalem and the Establishments of St. Louis and other tribunals held similar views.

I have been told of a witch cult in Southern Ireland practising nowadays, but I have not been able to contact it. The members are said to hold their meetings in a disused quarry where they can work without being disturbed. They wear long black cloaks for protection until they reach the meeting place, where they remove them to reveal a type of kilt made of two pieces of leather thonged at the sides. They are said to sacrifice animals to the moon, or at least to hold ceremonies in honour of the full moon, with dances regulated by a moon dial. I am told that they have one very beautiful dance, the Dance of the Four Winds, which is usually held round a standing stone or something which has four sides; but I can obtain no details. It is said that part of the initiation ceremony of the man is called Diana's Hunt, when all the single and unattached girls chase the initiate and whoever catches him beats him and then takes him under her guidance, it having usually been arranged beforehand who should catch him. I was told that blood was sometimes used in the rites and curses were put on people, but my informant knew nothing of the rites, or of their leader, except that there was a high priestess called Diana and that they use "whiskey".

The problem in investigating such a case is to find out whether the cult is an ancient one or whether it is of recent origin. In Ireland the people are either strongly Roman Catholic or just as strongly Protestant, and it is possible that someone may have invented a cult for fun, or in opposition to both religions. This, if it grew fairly strong, could not remain hidden for long, and then the Churches would be likely to combine to crush it. If, on the other hand, it had an ancient tradition, then it might have carried on, as its members would have realized the necessity for secrecy. The name Diana sounds a little like a modern invention; but from the Renaissance onwards there have been many classical scholars who might have applied this name to an ancient goddess.

There is a small town in Ireland where it is the custom every year to put in the market place a billy goat attended by two maidens for three days and nights; and during that time it is an open town. This is known as Puck Fair. The police stay in their stations, the public houses never close and no one goes to sleep, because that has always been the custom and it would bring bad luck to change it. This looks like the last of some curious pre-Christian religious rite which has survived.

If in Lady Alice's time there was a secret cult which brought luck to its votaries and curses upon its opponents, then it is not surprising to find it working today. In England, in their present form, the rituals and charges cannot be very old because they have been copied into modern language from grandfathers and grandmothers; but they do go back at least a hundred and fifty years. If they had been invented, then they would have been written in a sentimental form, whereas these are direct and to the point. Prior to 1800, when we know the cult was working, there was a certain interest in occult matters, but this was in the ceremonial type of magic, or the Hell Fire Club type, and these meant evoking the Devil. It is possible that someone may have started a new religion, but I think there must have been something already on which to graft it. I think it most curious that such a tradition should have come down from such early times. I have given my reasons for thinking that it must go back at least as far as the days of the first Elizabeth. If it was imported from Italy then, a relic of a Dionysian cult which had survived there, it could easily have survived in England; or it could have been imported from France by the Normans far earlier. I wonder if we shall ever really find out.

The people I know are taught never to use blood or to make sacrifices; but the Irish coven seemingly use them and they are used in Voodoo. Knowing how the rites in England work, these practices would be useless in any I know, so presumably there are totally different rites of which my friends know nothing.

The essence of magic is usually to raise power, then to use or control it. I can understand its being thought that killing something might release power or force, if the soul is force, but I do not understand how one would control or use it. Freshly shed blood might contain some vital power, which would exude slowly, and that blood might increase the power; but if this were the case, I should expect to hear that the municipal slaughter-house men were setting up as magicians. When I hear of this, I will believe in the power of blood. I know the Bacchantes were said to tear live animals to pieces and eat them, but I think they were people who, not understanding the occult teachings they received, mistook drunkenness for divine ecstasy, doing mad things in their frenzy. The law then restrained these excesses and reforms were carried out in the sect. The West Africans use blood, but, again, I think they do not have the true secrets.

CHAPTER X

WHAT ARE WITCHES?

Witches were the Wica or wise people, with herbal knowledge and a working occult teaching usually used for good—the author controverts Mr. Pennethorne Hughes concerning evil usages and poisons—witches cast spells to stop Hitler's landing—previous use of the same technique against Napoleon and the Spanish Armada—the killing of 9,000,000 witches—the part played by St. Dominic—the methods of Inquisitors: the use of torture—detailed account of tortures used in Germany—reports of victims' utterances under torture in Spain—Aldous Huxley's account of the torture to death of Grandier, 1634—the author repudiates the accusation that witches conduct a Black Mass—liberty still denied to witches, whose object is the release of ecstasy—use of herbs in this—the scandal of the Infamous Kiss—pacts with the Devil and accounts of them in the *Grimoires*—pacts between covens—contacts with other bodies in the 18th century—numerology of witches—two meanings of the word coven—these are smaller now—after the Norman conquest the local lord often figured as the Devil—the use of breath control and the ductless glands, herbs and poisons—the Pope makes surgery and witchcraft crimes—King Edward III and the witch origin of the Order of the Garter: two covens headed by the monarchs—the 168 letter S's on the King's robe—untruth of the charge that witches abjure Christianity—link with West Indian and Congo witches of today—witchcraft is hereditary—witches believe in gods who are not omnipotent and are pleased with man's being happy—quotation of verses "The Witch Remembers her Last Incarnation."

MR. HUGHES says: "Witchcraft proper only exists where the powers called upon are consciously felt to be evil ones, and those concerned in the operation are seeking aid from some force exterior to accepted conditions and beliefs." If this is true, then the witches of whom I have been speaking are not witches at all.

What are they then? They are the people who call themselves the Wica, the "wise people", who practise the age-old rites and who have, along with much superstition and herbal knowledge, preserved an occult teaching and working processes which they themselves think to be magic or witchcraft. They are the type of people who were burned alive for possessing this knowledge, often giving their lives to turn suspicion away from others. At Castletown we have a memorial to the nine million people who died by torture in one way or another for witchcraft.

These Wica generally work for good purposes and help

those in trouble to the best of their ability. Of course whatever
you do in this world you tread on someone's toes; if a witch
raised a good crop of corn in the old days, people complained
she was deflating the prices. I think it unwise to lay down the
law without knowing the subject.

Mr. Hughes goes on to say: "The physical powers of a witch
are those of a prehistoric people. How far good deeds done for
evil ends are permissible is a question for theologians." I think
the answer to this statement lies in the Jesuits' reported dictum:
"Evil deeds are always permissible for a good purpose, or when
they are to the benefit of the Order"—which is also a matter for
the theologians. I think the witch is justified in using any physical
power she has if it is used for the good of her community, provided she is injuring no one. Mr. Hughes says that the witch used
and sold poisons. Possibly; but the present-day ones have no real
knowledge of them. They know vaguely that hellebore is deadly,
as they know weed-killer is, but they do not know the correct
dose of either, and they do not know where to get hellebore. In
the Middle Ages whenever typhus fever broke out, as it did very
frequently, it was a stock thing to say the witches or the Jews
had poisoned the wells. Just because a witch may use a prehistoric cure to heal a sick child, it does not necessarily mean that
it is done for an evil end. Some individual witches may have
done wrong and evil things, but they are not the only ones
who can be blamed for that. The most obvious form of doing
evil is by sympathetic magic, the making of images. This is
done all over the world; if the victim knows it is being done
and firmly believes that it will kill him, then he can frighten
himself to death. A witch may make an image and frighten people
with it if they believe that she has the power to kill. Any person
may do it and the effect may be much the same, so this form of
evil is not exclusive to witchcraft. In 1318 the Bishop of Troyes
was tried, the evidence showing that he had made a wax image of
the Queen of France, and that after doing various indignities to
it, burned it, and so the Queen died!

Mr. Hughes goes on to say (page 146): "Witches cast spells,
they raised havoc, they poisoned, they aborted cattle and inhibited
human beings, they served the Devil, parodied Christian practices, allied themselves with the King's enemies, they copulated

with other witches in male and female form whom they took to be incubi or succubi; they committed abuses with domestic animals. More, they did these things consciously in the belief that they served a diabolical master and challenged heaven. Their motives were confused, their impulses were bemused, the proceedings more and more remote from any common original practices, yet they did them, and the reasons for what they did lie in the earliest religious beliefs."

I presume he thinks he knows what he is talking about, so let me reassure him that to the best of my knowledge most of these accusations are false. Witches did cast spells, to stop Hitler landing after France fell. They met, raised the great cone of power and directed the thought at Hitler's brain: "You cannot cross the sea," "You cannot cross the sea," "Not able to come," "Not able to come." Just as their great-grandfathers had done to Boney and their remoter forefathers had done to the Spanish Armada with the words: "Go on," "Go on," "Not able to land," "Not able to land." Is that allying themselves with the King's enemies? I am not saying that they stopped Hitler. All I say is that I saw a very interesting ceremony performed with the intention of putting a certain idea into his mind, and this was repeated several times afterwards; and though all the invasion barges were ready, the fact was that Hitler never even tried to come. The witches told me that their great-grandfathers had tried to project the same idea into Boney's mind.

At the time of the Spanish Armada the invading force was off the coast before the cult really heard about it. They knew it was useless trying to get at King Philip; he was out of touch with and could not change the Armada's course, and they had not the slightest idea who was in command. The only thing they could do was to send out a general idea: "Go on," "Go on," "Go on," "You cannot land," "You cannot land," and hope it would take effect. If they could have raised a storm, they would have done so, but they did not know how, though naturally they would pray to their gods to bring disaster to the fleet and this would probably include storms.

I doubt if witches ever raised havoc; at least I've never heard of their doing so, and I and they do not know how they would set about it; I would like information on the subject—dates and places, please? I cannot say no witch ever inhibited any human beings, or aborted cattle, any more than I can say no Bishop ever killed anyone by magic or poison. I have no knowledge of witches doing these things, but I do know of the Bishop of Troyes, and of the Borgia who was a Bishop before he was Pope. Copulating with incubi and domestic animals is just a bit of nasty nonsense, as is the charge that witches were serving a diabolical master. This was simply invented at the time of the persecutions, when judges would not convict and so the Church had to make up some crime that would warrant death. Witches have their own gods and they believe they are good; what more can any Christian say? There may be confusion or, rather, slight differences between the rituals and practices in different covens, I do not know; but do, for instance, the practices of the British Israelites, the Mormons, the Calathumpians and the Plymouth Brethren form one harmonious whole? Yet are they not all of the Christian faith?

In the era of terror, just after the disastrous Children's Crusade, Pope Innocent III made surgery a crime. He denounced the old pre-Christian faith as heresy and witchcraft and set the Inquisition to crush it.

About nine million people suffered death by torture. The Dominicans, founded by St. Dominic, a devoted ascetic who whipped himself three times daily and used to pluck birds alive, were put in charge of the persecutions, and they spread the story of a conspiracy against Christ. Some people say they really believed some of the things they preached, but this I find hard to credit, though the more ignorant of their hearers might. It is certain that from the orgy of persecution, as in the earlier cases of persecutions against the various sects of heretics, someone obtained enormous loot, and, of course, it is true that these people were guilty of worshipping their own god in their own way.

Some people say that the Church simply had written lists, and tortured witches and Knights Templar till they said "Yes" to all charges, and this accounts for all resemblances. But this is only partly true. The important resemblances are not in the stock charges, but in little, unimportant things, and many of these resemble what is still done today in Africa, America and Madagascar, of which the Inquisitors had no knowledge. The fact is, the average person can tell a big lie, but cannot invent all the little details to deceive a good cross-examiner and so lets out bits of seemingly unimportant truth.

That is why soldiers if captured are told to give only their name, rank and number: not to try and deceive the enemy by giving false information, because in doing so they usually give out some true facts which help him.

Officers are taught to question prisoners, to pick out bits of truth from wildly impossible stories. Inquisitors were expert cross-examiners, but did not always realize the importance of little details that came out. Their business was to weed out heresy, and they did this thoroughly.

It is often said that witches have confessed to the most abominable practices. This is quite true, but it must be remembered why they did so. Paul Carus in *The History of the Devil*, page 323 (Archives of the International Folk Lore Association), calls the *Malleus Maleficorum,* or *Witch-Hammer*, the most infamous work ever written. It advises beginning a trial with the question "whether or not the person on trial believes in witchcraft", and adds: "mind that witches generally deny the question." If the culprit denies, then the inquisitor continues: "Well then, whenever witches are burnt, they are innocently condemned." A denial of witchcraft sealed the doom of the accused at once, for, according to the *Witch-Hammer*, "the greatest heresy is not to believe in witchcraft" (*haeresis est maxima opera maleficorum non credere*). However, if the accused affirmed the question, torture made him confess. To plead ignorance was of no avail, for the refusal of a confession was counted a crime under the name *maleficium taciturnitatis*. There was no escape, and the best course for the victim on the rack was to confess all at once without a relapse into denials, for that at least abbreviated the procedure. According to page 330, "before the torture began, the accused was forced to drink the witch-broth, a disgusting concoction mixed with the ashes of burnt witches, and supposed to protect the torturers against the evil influence of witchcraft."

The filth (*carceris squaloris*) of the dungeons was used. The same page tells of the torture applied to a woman in the year 1631 on the first day of her trial.

Unfortunately he does not give the place, or whether it was

by the Inquisition or the Reformed Church; but this is a translation from Konig, *Ausgeburten des Menschenwahns*, p. 130; also
Soldan, *Hexenprocesse*, p. 269-70.

"(1) The hangman binds the woman, who was pregnant,
and places her on the rack. Then he racked her till her heart
would fain break. . . .

(2) When she did not confess, the torture was repeated . . .
he cut off her hair, poured brandy over her head and burned it.

(3) He placed sulphur in her armpits and burned it.

(4) Her hands were tied behind her, she was hauled up to
the ceiling and suddenly dropped down.

(5) This hauling up and dropping down was repeated for
some hours, till the hangman and his helpers went to dinner.

(6) When they returned her feet and hands were tied
upon her back; brandy was poured on her back and burned.

(8) Then heavy weights were placed on her back and
she was pulled up.

(9) After this she was again stretched on the rack.

(10) A spiked board was placed on her back, and she
again was hauled up to the ceiling.

(11) The master again ties her feet and hangs on them a
block of fifty pounds. . . .

(12) The master . . . fixes her legs in a vice, tightening the
jaws until the blood oozes out from the toes.

(13) She was stretched and pinched again in various ways.

(14) Now the hangman of Dreissigacker began the third
grade of torture. (Note: No indication of what he did.)

(15) The hangman's son-in-law hauled her up to the
ceiling by her hands.

(16) The hangman . . . whipped her with a horsewhip.

(17) She was placed in a vice where she remained for six
hours.

(18) She was mercilessly horsewhipped.

All this was done on the first day."

(Note: They have left out No. 7 from this list. I do not
suppose it was any less painful than the others.)

From *Archivob Hist. Nacional, Inquisicion de Tolado*, Leg. 138,
quoted in H. C. Lea *History of the Inquisition of Spain*, Vol. III,

p. 24. Reports taken of the Examination under torture. After long torture the inquisitor would say: "Tell all."

"If I knew what to say, I would say it. Oh, Senor, I don't know what I have to say. Oh, Oh! they are killing me—if they would tell me what—Oh, Senores, Oh, my heart, . . . loosen me and I will tell the truth; I don't know what I have to tell—loosen me for the sake of God—tell me what I have to say—I did it, I did it—they hurt me, Senor—loosen me, loosen me and I will tell it . . . I don't know what I have to tell—Senor, I did it. . . . Take me from here and tell me, what I have to say. . . . I don't remember, tell me what I have to say—O wretched me; I will tell all that is wanted, Senors—they are breaking my arms—loosen me a little—I did everything that is said of me. . . . What am I wanted to tell? I did everything—loosen me, for I don't remember what I have to tell. . . . Oh, Oh, Oh, tell all." And again the cruel voice would say: "Tell all."

When a poor wretch was tortured enough, they would dictate to him what to say, and whom to implicate. The average person conveniently forgets that this was done, if indeed he ever knew; but witches do not forget that this or similar treatment was meted out to their ancestors, and the days of persecution are not over, at least in many places, so the witch still keeps underground.

Aldous Huxley in his most enlightening book *The Devils o, Loudun* tells (page 177) of the tortures and death of one Grandier in 1634 on the charge of bewitching some nuns. The particulars are taken from the Court Records and are authentic:

"In the presence of two apothecaries and several doctors Grandier was stripped, shaved all over and then systematically pricked to the bone with a long, sharp probe . . . the pain was excruciating and, through the bricked-up windows, the prisoner's screams could be heard by the ever-growing crowd of the curious in the street below. In the official summary of the counts on which Grandier was condemned, we learn that owing to the great difficulty in locating such small areas of insensibility, only two out of the five marks described by the Prioress were actually discovered . . . Mannoury's methods, it may be added, were admirably simple and effective. After a score of agonizing jabs he would reverse the probe and press the blunt end against the person's flesh. *Miraculously, there was no pain, the devil had marked the spot.* Had he been permitted to go on long enough, there is no doubt that Mannoury would have discovered all the marks. Unfortunately, one of the apothecaries (an untrustworthy stranger from Tours) was less complacent than the village doctors whom Loubardemont had assembled to control the experiment. Catching Mannoury in the act of cheating, the man protested, in vain. His minority report was merely ignored. Meanwhile, Mannoury and the others had proved themselves most gratifyingly co-operative."

Page 235: "The judges saw the defendant only three times in all. Then, after the usual pious preliminaries they rendered their decision; it was unanimous. Grandier was to be subjected to the 'Question', Ordinary and Extraordinary . . . With a rope round his neck and a two-pound taper in his hand, ask pardon of God, the King and Justice . . . then burnt alive. . . . He was stripped, in a few minutes his body was hairless . . . 'his moustache and little beard, now eyebrows,' said the Commissioner. 'Now the fingernails, you will now pull out the fingernails. . . .' "

Page 244: "He was bound stretched out on the floor, his legs from knees to feet enclosed between four boards, of which the outer pair were fixed, the inner ones movable. By driving wedges into the space between the two movable boards it was possible to crush the victim's legs . . . the first wedge was driven home between the knees, then another was inserted at the feet. When this was hammered to the head . . . a third was inserted immediately below the first. . . . At the second stroke of the fourth wedge several bones of the feet and ankles were broken . . . a fifth wedge was inserted. The prisoner asked: 'Father, do you believe on your conscience a man ought merely to be delivered from pain, to confess a crime he has not committed' . . . 'you have been a magician, you have had commerce with devils' was the answer. When he protested once more he was innocent, the sixth wedge was hammered home, then a seventh, then an eighth; the bones of the knees, the shins, the ankles and feet, all were shattered."

Page 249: "The two-pound taper was placed in Grandier's hand and he was lifted down from the cart to beg pardon, as the sentence had prescribed, for his crime, but there were no knees to kneel on. When they lowered him to the ground, he fell forward on his face."

He was finally burnt alive, care being taken to see that his death was a most painful one.

After the lesser people were liquidated, the persecution turned to where there was more loot still to be found, and among others the Knights Templar, who had done so much for Christendom, were charged with heresy, with many of the stock charges and with unnatural vice. How far they, or some of them, were technically guilty is ground for dispute, but very many were doubtless innocent of any conscious heresy.

Mr. Hughes goes on to say that the witch cult conducted a Black Mass where Christian practices were ridiculed and the Devil received homage and praise. Again, let me assure him that though I have been to many sabbats I have seen nothing resembling the practices he accuses us of, unless he is thinking of the ceremony of the "cakes and wine" which may be an imitation of the ancient Christian *Agape*, the love feast, though I think it is much older. I do not say that the Black Mass has never been celebrated, but I do say that it is not done by witches, to the best of my knowledge.

We must accept the fact that, though the cult is very interesting and in part extremely fine, it is primitive, and when people "let loose" in any community, then things are bound to happen and they do things which they would not normally do on their own. This is doubtless very distressing to the Puritans; but then Puritans rather glory in being "distressed" at things and I can see the witches' point of view.

We talk a great deal of religious freedom, of our rights, and the liberty of the subject, but we still deny all liberty to witches. They are still persecuted just because some snooper was shocked by finding people in some lonely place dancing naked round a fire at night many hundreds of years ago. People are still being shocked these days at what they see on the beaches and elsewhere, and rush to the newspapers to complain, but they are usually laughed at for their pains. Beaches are public property and people may have a right to complain, but the sabbat was a private party and they could only have been seen by people snooping in the hope of being shocked. Witches have for hundreds of years held their meetings in private; they are people who want release from this world into the world of fantasy. To certain kinds of person the relief gained has been of enormous benefit and these occasional nights of release are something to live for. Among primitive people dancing was the usual religious expression. In witch tradition it was the necessary preliminary to the climax of the sabbat, the producing of power; it may have had other objects, to bring joy and to express beauty. This was Sin to what Chesterton called "that gang of revolting Calvinists", though St. Thomas Aquinas only says: "All dancers are not necessarily damned." Some people may have blundered into a sabbat and been shocked, but the Anglo-Saxons are notorious for being easily shocked and complaining to the powers that be.

I am told that in the olden days witches had knowledge of a herb called Kat which, when mixed with incense, would release the inner eye, the subconscious, but unless another herb, Sumach, was mixed with it, it could not be used for long as it would produce hallucinations. If you used both correctly, it was possible to leave the body. Unfortunately they do not know what these herbs were; but both are said to grow in England. It is said that if man breathes incense with Kat in it, then woman becomes more beautiful, so it is possible that it contained wild hemp. Sorcerers used something for the same purpose and their mixture contained hemp and many other ingredients to tone it down. Many primitive races use drugs to obtain elevation of the spirits, Coca in South America, Peyotl in Mexico and many other substances. They have a varying effect on the nervous system, bringing about what might be the opening of the inner eye or perhaps hallucinations. Alcohol has the effect of increasing precognition, as the Society for Psychical Research records prove.

Another charge made against witches, the Templars, the Waldenses, the Gnostics and many others was the "Osculum Infame". This may have been a stock charge against anyone the clerics disliked, and seems to have been used on the principle that any stick is good enough to beat a dog with. It was first used against all the various sects of heretics, then against the Knights Templar. Witches do not kiss the Devil's posterior, first because they never kiss anyone's posterior and, secondly, because the Devil is never there for anyone to kiss. I cannot make it any clearer than that, can I? As I have said, there is no pact with the Devil or with anyone else. This, I think, arose from the Faust type of legend which may have been coined by clerics to frighten people from thinking of engaging in magical practices, or possibly to explain why people who performed magical experiments of the more or less permitted Key of Solomon type, without using a medium, usually did not succeed.

These stories were usually fabricated in order to boost the power of some saint and were to the effect that a sorcerer, after years of failure, had made a pact with the Devil, selling his soul for so many years of wealth and power. When his time came he prayed to the particular saint, who called up the Devil and by force or trickery got the pact back. The sorcerer then promptly gave all the profits of his sorcery to the saint's shrine and died in an odour of sanctity. The story of these pacts is rather naive, but there was a belief in them, and *Grimoires*, textbooks of semi-Black Magic, were printed, professing to tell one how to raise the Devil and conclude a pact with him, and at the same time to trick him. This was usually done by a play of words, giving him your body and soul, whether you be buried inside or outside the church, and then getting buried inside the church wall, that is, neither inside nor outside—in other words, cheating him. They seemed actually to have thought that the Devil was too simple or too ignorant to buy the book and read it for himself.

Since writing the above, I have read of a trial in France, where a clerk was employed by a mysterious man dressed in black to copy one of these books. It was seriously alleged in court that this man in black was the Devil, trying to obtain a copy of this book, to learn how to safeguard himself against such trickery. The accused was found guilty of attempting to aid the Devil and was executed. This shows how childish were some of the charges, resembling the sort of thing the Nazis and the Communists accused people of doing, and getting confessions in the same way by the most atrocious tortures. I suppose these books were sold to the type of people who believe nowadays in sixpenny fortune-telling pamphlets; they were made to sell, and the most famous among them was the *Grimoire* of Pope Honorius.

The whole question of belief in such pacts intrigues me, because a certain number of specimens do exist. It would seem that the belief was that at the last day, as at a great trial, the soul swore that it had never used any sorcery; it was on the point of gaining Heaven, when suddenly a Devil would produce the missing document from his files. It would be admitted as evidence, proved to be the accused's signature, and the Devil would win the case and the soul.

Now each coven is independent, and during the fierce persecution the members of some of them may have used some sort of pact to bind them together; but this would not have had any diabolical associations, if only because this would have had the most disastrous results if found. Again, when the Hell Fire Clubs were in vogue amongst freethinkers two hundred years ago, it is just possible that there were some witches among those who attended them, and that they may have helped to make up some of the ritual which was a bit of fooling and which included pacts. But it is as true that there may have been butchers and bakers and candlestick-makers who might have done the same; that would not mean that all members of these trades concluded pacts with the Devil. Members of these Clubs might have been interested in things phallic, as they interested Aleister Crowley fifty years ago. He belonged to the witch cult; he certainly knew about it and he may have had some hand in reconstructing rituals. If he did, he kept his oaths of secrecy and never gave a hint of it away in any of his many writings.

In ancient times probably many magicians, amongst the scholars and learned men, before and during the fall of Byzantium, came West and many may have made contact with the cult; also men who read forbidden books would be apt to come to the only places where they could meet people with free minds, the houses of the witches. Later Rosicrucians and Freemasons might have attended. They might not have known that their hosts were witches in all cases, though they would have known there were places where they might discuss things reasonably without fear of being tortured and burnt. There are resemblances to Free-masonry in certain parts of the rites which I think cannot be due to chance, so I think the one influenced the other. And it is probable that all these people may have brought some new ideas into the cult; but I think the only great changes were made in Roman times when contact was made with the mysteries, although this is all guesswork on my part. I can only judge on the evidence I can find.

The cult seems to use a crude numerology—whence obtained I do not know. The numbers 3, 5, 8, 13 and 40 are thought good or lucky and all these numbers have significance attached to them. There are three working tools which are essential and nothing can be done without them; that is, something to cut and stab with, something to strike with and something to bind with. There are five others, all of which have their special uses and are only needed if that particular kind of work is being done. For an initiation all eight must be present and the initiate is told the use of, and holds, each in turn. Because three and five make eight, many things must be in eights; but eight and five make thirteen, so thirteen is another good number; but since five eights, or three covens and a leader, make forty, forty is a good number and certain things must be forty. The coven traditionally consists of twelve witches and a leader, probably because it is a lucky number and because there are thirteen moons in a year.

I think I must make this clear: that the word *coven* is used in two senses. First, it is a band which may be of any number of initiated people who have a common leader, who hold meetings and celebrate the rites. The leader may be a man or a woman, but a high priestess (whom they may borrow from another coven, if they have not got one of their own available) must be present to celebrate the rites. In the old days there were numbers of people who would come to the meetings who were of the faith but were uninitiated (not received into the circle, or taught the secrets). I think that in the old days there was no real secrecy about what the initiation consisted of; anyone could see and hear it much as one may see a baptism or marriage. But unless you undergo the marriage or baptismal rites you are not married or baptized; neither does knowing how a marriage is performed give you power to marry someone else.

Secondly, a coven can also mean the people who celebrate the rites in the circle. Traditionally, this consists of six perfect couples and a leader; preferably the couples are husbands and wives, or at least betrothed. That is, they should be lovers, in sympathy with each other, as this gives the best results. They can give me no reason for this number of thirteen, except custom and that "more would make the rite too long, as each has to do certain things in turn". Also six couples and a leader is the most that can work in a nine-foot circle—and you do not become giddy so easily in a larger one. These dances are intoxicating, and this intoxication is the condition for producing what they call magic. The only time I have seen a larger circle used was when we tried to work on Hitler's mind, and that was a totally different operation: "Sending Forth", performed in an entirely different way, needing as many people as we could get together and plenty of room to work in.

In these degenerate days six perfect couples are not always available, so others are taken in to make up the numbers. These are all "purified" as soon as they enter the circle; other initiates present, and children, would sit outside and watch the proceedings. Later these would probably be purified and taken into the circle to receive the sacred meal. When the rites in the circle were finished, all would join in the feast and dance. If there were, say, twenty initiates present with two qualified priestesses and there was enough room, they tell me they might form two covens and have two circles, with one common leader to keep them in time, and that in the old days at large meetings in the open air they might have many such circles; but I have never seen more than one. Nowadays numbers are so few that practically everyone comes into the circle, though I have seen a man sit outside, refusing to come in because his girl was not there that night.

They tell me that in the old days they often used to choose the prettiest young girl suitable to represent the goddess at large meetings. She was known as the Maiden. She was made a sort of acting high priestess and treated with the greatest honour and would often act as sort of hostess to distinguished visitors (i.e. the Devil if he turned up), but the real power remained in the hands of the true priestess, who usually worked all the magic. Often the Maiden was the high priestess's daughter and would take the place of her mother in time and there was sometimes some mystification over this; seeing the resemblance at a distance

ignorant visitors believed that the high priestess became young
again at the meetings.

They say that in the old days there were rules that there
must not be more than one large coven in a certain area, so as to
prevent arguments as to who should belong to whom; but they
are uncertain about these rules now. It is certain that long ago
there was some sort of central authority, exercised by a common
leader, whom the Church called the Devil, but they know
nothing of this nowadays and would not know how to recognize
him if he turned up. They have no regular system of passwords,
that I could discover, to recognize each other by. But at initiations there are certain words required to pass you into the circle,
and there are certain catchphrases that could be used as such; of
course a knowledge of the mysteries would prove you were
initiated. Actually, they all know each other, or are introduced, so
they do not need passwords.

In Italy witches are said to say "six and seven" as a password,
because it would be dangerous to say thirteen; these numbers
of course add up to thirteen.

In England I could understand their saying five and eight for
the same reason, but actually they mostly know each other in the
coven and so do not need passwords; they very often do not
know of the existence of other covens.

*   *   *   *   *

In ancient times at least the leaders were always of the old
races—the people with the natural powers of hypernormal
control of the body by simple auto-intoxication. As the Normans
began to form alliance with the people of the heaths, some of
them, probably those who had an inherited witch tradition, seem
to have taken office. It would be, of course, the most intelligent
of the Normans, perhaps those with fairy wives, who lived with
the people of the heaths but whose children might come to the
towns. Then the mixed race thus formed seems to have taken
over some of the priestly functions. They probably had to work
hard to condition their bodies to obtain the results which came
easily to their mothers, but would at least have some power. The
Normans were politically minded and as they realized they were

losing political power, to prevent themselves from being entirely submerged in the new nationalism they infiltrated into the old cult. These never attained the same powers of hypernormal control as the older race, but the mixed breed vastly improved their own race. The town-dweller thus had his own priesthood, which had most of the old traditional knowledge; but the great priests would still be among the people of the heaths, well known to all.

Often a mysterious masked figure, sometimes dressed in skins and with horns, would appear at the great ceremonies. Most likely it was whispered that he was a great lord, though the more ignorant might think he was a god or devil. Actually he probably would be an important Norman, who protected the people of the heath in everyday life. As an important visitor he would be hospitably entertained and act as the mate of the local high priestess, who was possibly his fairy wife.

In all probability there would be a large congregation of the people of the heath and also there would be many of the local people, the farming, cattle-keeping or fisherman type, who, although perhaps nominally Christian, attended the seasonal dances in honour of the old religion and practised the more or less recognized fertility rites, much as they attended church services or danced round the maypole. These were not really witches in any sense; fertility was what they wanted. "Good crops, good fishing, good luck." They would attend the meetings of any god who was good to them, and "goodness" to them was the quality of one who helped you when in trouble and who had merry festivals. They were no theologians. A good life now and a good life in the next world were enough for them: it didn't matter what the god's name was. The secret of who the masked man was would be kept from them. There would also be a number of the gentry, lesser nobles, or their sons and daughters and many of the clever artisan class who, not rich, were at least comfortably off and lived much better than their neighbours. Many of these, perhaps, did not bring their wives unless they were of the fairy stock or were broadminded and enjoyed the fun. But if their daughters were of the "bright young things" type they would come, possibly to father's disgust. Some at least of these would be initiated; but if they wanted release into the ecstatic state they would have to obtain the help of someone of the old stock; in other words, "go to a witch". That is, they might know or guess the formula, from seeing it done, but they had not the special short cuts nor the long and arduous spiritual discipline to sublimate the body and isolate the spirit.

They may have guessed what even witches knew vaguely, that there were certain parts of the body, some of which nowadays we speak of as the ductless glands and the spinal ganglia, which could be stimulated. They knew of breath control and that the slowing down of the blood supply in certain parts, and the stimulating of it in others, would produce certain results, and that concentration and a firm, unquestioning belief, or suggestion, all had effects. Perhaps they did not recognize where one began and the other ended, but they used them all together and called and thought of them all as "the craft", or magic. They also knew there were certain incenses which aided this concentration to develop spiritual vision and induce a clairvoyant state.

In mediaeval times many ingredients came from the Near East, but originally the most potent herbs seem to have been local ones, and among these some were poisonous. This knowledge of poisons, as I have said, is not necessarily evil; it is how that knowledge is used that matters. To use it to gain a trance state harms no one except yourself. But as a weaker people are sometimes tempted to use these methods against oppressors, poison would occasionally be used by them. That it was not done on any large scale is proved by the fact that there was no large death-roll among the active persecutors of the witches.

Whilst England was at best but semi-Christian, this happy state of give and take prevailed. The parish priest in the country districts winked at what happened; he often attended the merrymakings himself. Priests and even Bishops often performed fertility rites themselves. If a priest put on a mask and went to the dances he might be unknown—or he might be well known and not care.

When the State religion became officially and truly Christian, and the Church had obtained real power, these goings-on were frowned upon; all respectable folk were expected to conform to Christian principles, at least in public, and slowly this came to pass. The respectable folk knew all about the happenings on the

heath, but they regarded them much as the good burghers of
Scotland did the Highlanders 300 years ago—as a horrid, godless,
plundering clan, with whom no respectable person "south of the
Highland Line" would admit having relations. But these same
respectable people traded with them, bought stolen cattle from
them, asked them for help when in trouble, took refuge with
them, and even intermarried with them and were quite proud of
their relationship. When they went north of this line, the younger
members of the community, in search of adventure or sweethearts,
often went among these impossible people, and I think it was
much this way too in England prior to 1220.

When the Pope made surgery and witchcraft crimes, practically everyone knew who was who, and the destruction of the
Little People was easy. Then the town witches' turn came. These
were easy, too, for they were the people who lived well and were
worth looting. The majority were exterminated by various forms
of torture. But they were also the people most valuable to the
community, the people who made things, the blacksmith and the
builder among others, the farmers who grew the food. The
nobles probably protected those whom they could, but many
nobles were themselves attacked and convicted, as was the
Duchess of Gloucester and Margery Jourdemain, the Witch of
Eye.

It is said that King Edward III saved one witch from certain
torture at that famous incident to which the origin of the Order
of the Garter was ascribed. He was dancing with the Countess of
Salisbury when she dropped the ritual Garter which proclaimed
her high rank in the cult. With Bishops about this was dangerous,
so the King, knowing what it was, picked it up and put it on his
own leg, saying: "Honi soit qui mal y pense." The mid-Victorians,
to whom a garter was slightly naughty, made pretty Christmas
cards of the "Blushing Countess"; but ladies of those times, and
this lady in particular, were hard-boiled; it took more than a garter
to make them blush. The King's quickness saved the situation
and placed him almost in the position of their incarnate god in the
eyes of his more pagan subjects. This was followed by the foundation of an Order of twelve Knights for the King and twelve for
the Prince of Wales, i.e. twenty-six members in all, or two covens.
Froissart's words imply that Edward perfectly understood the

underlying meaning of the Garter, for he says: "The King told them it should prove an excellent expedient for uniting not only his subjects one with another but all foreigners conjunctively with them in the bonds of amity and peace." Dr. Murray points out that the King's mantle as chief of the Order was powdered over with one hundred and sixty-eight garters, which together with his own, worn on the leg, makes one hundred and sixty-nine, or thirteen times thirteen: that is, thirteen covens. I am told that long ago witches sometimes did have as many circles às this, with one common leader or timekeeper. It is noteworthy also that the Black Book containing the institution of the Garter was taken away and destroyed not long after his death. I have seen two witch garters; they were of green snakeskin with gold or silver gilt buckles and were backed with blue silk. They were worn above the left knee. They are badges of rank.

In this connection, can anyone tell me exactly what is the meaning of the double SS on the collar of the Garter? It is sometimes said to mean the Virgin, sometimes the Holy Ghost (*Sanctus Spiritus*). The Order is dedicated to the Virgin, certainly, but I do not see how it can refer to her. Nor does it seem to be dedicated to the Holy Ghost. My reason for asking is that on all Athama and many other witch tools I have seen—and I have seen many besides those in my own private collection—there are a number of signs carved. These are always the same and in the same order and have the same meanings. It is necessary to have these signs put on before they are consecrated. (In the burning times they would write them in ink and wash them off after consecration.) The third sign is SS: that is, two S's as used on the collar of the Garter. Witches have their own interpretation of this sign (and it is not the Virgin or the Holy Ghost).

Black is said to be a feature in the Order of the Garter. The Black Book, containing the original constitutions of the Order, is said to have been taken away for secret reasons before the time of Henry V, as mentioned earlier, and from this Black Book comes the important post of Black Rod. One would think that there must have been important reasons to conceal something before such a book could be taken away or lost. The late Hargrave Jennings seemed convinced that there was some deep mystery here, but he apparently did not know, or if he did he did not mention this witch mark, which is also shown in the Key of Solomon. All this may be purely coincidence, and coincidence killed the Professor. But if no one mentions coincidences, there is little chance of finding further facts; and there is the undoubted fact that the garter is a badge of rank among witches, and further there is a prehistoric rock drawing in France supposed to represent a magical witch ceremony, twelve women dancing round a man who is stark naked except for garters. As stockings were not worn for several thousand years afterwards, these must have some meaning.

After the fierce persecutions it was generally impossible to hold the great rites, and they were only very occasionally celebrated. As the religious motives lessened, the rites were practised mainly by people who had an urge towards mystic learning, and as it was no longer possible to raise power in the grand and easy way other means to this end were cultivated. Besides the formula, it is necessary to have some innate power of hyperaesthesia or prevision which can be developed with practice. In the olden days one would see examples everywhere and know positively how it worked and could easily obtain the necessary herbs; and nowadays, even though everything is against it, this practice still goes on.

A very common but untrue charge against witches was that initiates were required to abjure Christianity. At the initiation a long charge was read which told the candidate what would be required of him; but there was no question of giving up any other faith. He was told that he would obtain benefits and help in the future life by the aid of the goddess, who asked nothing in return. The pact with the Devil is nonsense; the only promise is one of secrecy and to help one's brothers and sisters when in need. One has to be formally introduced to the coven, though in name one is introduced to the Mighty Ones—the spirits of the dead members of the cult who have not been reincarnated and who are supposed to be present. I can see no real reason why one cannot be a good enough though unorthodox Christian and a witch at the same time. It seems to me easier than being a Christian and a Communist. The Christian who thinks reincarnation heresy, who will not countenance any form of superstition and belongs to the Sabbath Day Observance League, would certainly not make a good witch. It is possible that the grandfathers of some of these people may have called their leader the Devil in the days when it was considered rather advanced to talk of the Devil. It may be argued that many witches confessed to signing pacts. Of course they did, and so would I if I were tortured long enough. Recent experiments by the Nazis have proved that people can be made to say anything under torture. By confessing to dealings with the Devil they were quickly condemned and burnt, but they avoided giving away essentials. They confessed to using charms to gain good harvests, without mentioning the methods used, and always delighted in telling of the joyous side which was anathema to the religious.

It is noticeable that much of what our witches confessed to is borne out by the practices of the West Indian and Congo witches of today, and that things told by Arabian writers of long ago are practised by witches in Madagascar today. I think this must be more than coincidence.

In early days very many children were brought up as witches. It was a recognized fact that it was an hereditary cult, and therefore children were often executed with their mothers. In England in 1718, a witch, Mrs. Huke, was hanged along with her nine-year-old child, just as a witch burnt in Castletown died with her young son, the only reason being that he was the son of a witch. The Puritans were strong in the Isle of Man at that time and so obtained a conviction. At other times the Bishops complained that it was impossible to get a Manx jury to convict witches, so they were usually put in the Bishop's Prison under Peel Castle until they died of cold and starvation. The Manx had a soft spot for witches, for they gave good medicines and love charms and they were, until Methodism came in, very highly respected.

Most of them were born into the cult, but sometimes outsiders were recruited from those wishing to gain occult powers, from those who came from curiosity, and I think mainly from those who fell in love with a member. Membership of the cult meant torture and death if discovered, but it promised certain times of happiness, a partial release from the everyday round of toil and boredom, and rest and comradeship with rebirth for those who still loved this world—in fact a chance of good things in this world, and a saving from purgatory and Hell in the next.

They firmly believed in this and therefore risked initiating their children. If these betrayed you, it meant torture and death for you. If they kept faith, someone else might yet betray them, with like result. But some of them thought more of the future life and the promise: "If steadfast you go to the pyre, drugs will reach you, you will feel naught, you will but go to death and what lies beyond, the ecstasy of the goddess."

The faith of the cult is summed up in a witch's book I possess which states that they believed in gods who were not all-powerful. They wished men well, they desired fertility for man and beast and crops, but to attain this end they needed man's help. Dances and other rites gave this help. These rites were based on sympathetic magic, the idea that like attracts like, and also that "what gave pleasure to man, gave pleasure to the gods". Possibly they thought that the gods could feel man's pleasure. There was also the idea that the gods loved man and were pleased when he was happy, as opposed to the idea that god is an angry god who hates man to be happy. In this book are the following verses, but no indication of who wrote them:

The Witch Remembers her Last Incarnation

I remember, O fire,
  How thy flames once enkindled my flesh,
Among writhing witches caught close in thy flame,
  Now tortured for having beheld what is secret.
But to those who saw what we had seen
  Yea, the fire was naught.
Ah well I remember the buildings ablaze
  With the light that our bodies had lit.
And we smiled, to behold the flames wind about us,
  The faithful, among the faithless and blind.
To the chanting of prayers
  In the frenzy of flame
We sang hosannas to Thee, our Gods,
Midst the strength-giving fire,
  Pledged our love to Thee from the Pyre.

I think this shows what they believed. It is very often said: Oh, but witches were only executed because they were poisoners. Now I freely admit that there have been some cases of suspected poisoning, where witchcraft was also alleged; there have also been some cases of witchcraft where poisoning was alleged. But there were very few of these; most of the cases were simply that witchcraft was alleged, either because there was some cause to suspect some connection with heresy, with fairies, or with forbidden knowledge, or because of personal spite, non-attendance at church, not giving enough money to the Church, or simply because they were people who were worth looting. Those were the discreditable reasons why they were convicted.

CHAPTER XI

SOME OTHER MATTERS

Details of the modern coven and its circle—curious absence of the Cup from the witches' working tools—substitution of censer and pentacle—witches cannot "work" the weather, but they do have clairvoyant power and observations about weather—periods of history that have suited witches: Athens, perhaps ancient Crete and Egypt—in Celtic times they had great scope, but opposition in Rome—the obscuration of witchcraft by Kabbalistic magic in Renaissance times—Italian and ptomaine poisoning blamed on witches—a wax image of Elizabeth—was the Earl of Bothwell head of the Scottish witches?—modern witchcraft doomed because of changed conditions.

I THINK that I must make it clear that, as far as my experience goes, while the coven should traditionally have six couples and a leader in the circle, nowadays it may often have less. At a meeting, if there were more than thirteen initiated people present they would sit outside with any uninitiated and watch the religious rite. If for certain reasons they were required in the circle, others would step outside to make room, and those without would then be purified and taken inside. When the rites were finished and the circle closed, all took part in the dance and feast. If there were, say, twenty initiated and enough room, they would probably form two covens, each in their own circle, with one leader or timekeeper. If there were still more, they would form three circles. Nowadays, no uninitiated persons are ever present and the ceremonies are usually indoors, where there is seldom room for more than one circle. Also, though the witch ideal is to form perfect couples of people ideally suited to each other and so in perfect sympathy, and to cause people to be suited to each other, nowadays this is not always possible; the right couples go together, the others go singly and make do as they can. Witchcraft today is largely a case of "make do".

Another matter I must explain. At first I was puzzled by the absence of the Cup from the witches' working tools and the inclusion of the unimportant pentacle, said to be used to com-

mand spirits; also that while the witches admittedly used a
form of spiritualism, asking departed spirits to return or communicate, they did not generally evoke—that is, command—
either spirits or Elementals to appear, and then, by commands,
bribes or sacrifices, cause them to do services. The more so
because, through their connection with sorcerers, they knew
of these practices. Also, in the explanation of the working
tools, mention is made of such matters. The answer I get is:
In the burning times this was done deliberately. Any mention
of the Cup led to an orgy of torture, their persecutors saying that
it was a parody of the Mass; also the riding or dancing pole
("broomstick") was cut out. Censer and pentacle were sub-
stituted and explanations made to fit what their persecutors
expected. If all told more or less the same story of what they
were taught—because it was actually true and it agreed with
the story of others—why bother to continue the torture? The
witch was convicted, and if she did not escape or die in prison,
she was quickly burnt and her troubles were over. It was the
poor wretch who was not an initiated witch who was tortured
and tortured again and again, because she did not know what
to say and could not invent a story that would pass muster.
This explanation is I think plausible. Naturally, at times, individual witches may have attempted to work with elementals, but
the general feeling is: "These are usually evil, it is unlucky to
have dealings with them, and the goddess is sweet and kind and
would not like it. It is wrong to go against her teachings." Of
course, I am only speaking about the witches belonging to the
cult. The village wise-woman fortune-telling type may have done
anything.

Witches are constantly accused of raising storms. My informants simply do not know how to, and, by the system of magic
they use, I do not see how they could, except of course by asking
their gods. In other words, *"by prayer"*. They know vaguely that
pouring water, especially over a naked virgin, is said to produce
rain, but they have no special rite or ceremonial to that effect, or
if they had, it has not been preserved. In both the First and Second
World Wars there were stories that the Germans could and did
work the weather to their own advantage, and witches wondered
if this was true, and if so, how it was done. Undoubtedly

in the old days part of the witches' job was to work the weather, but this seems to have been done on witch-doctor lines: by their clairvoyant powers and observation they knew when rain was coming and only started rain-making when they knew it was on the way. Again, they knew if a long drought was coming and could advise farmers accordingly. If fine harvesting weather could be expected, they told the farmer to let the crops ripen; if rain was coming, to call all hands to get the crops in and to get the roofs ready in case of impending storm. They did not consider this charlatanism. As they say, half of their power came from people who believed in them and so would take their advice. If people knew how it was done they would say: "Oh, we'll try it too"; one would work against the other and it would be chaos. The witch wants quiet, regular, ordinary good government with everyone content and happy, plenty of fun and games when you are alive, all fear of death being taken away; as you grow older, you rather welcome the idea of death, as an abode of peace and rest, where you grow young again, ready to return for another round on earth.

Unfortunately, few periods of history have suited witches. I think personally that at Athens their system, or some system like theirs, had great success in spite of the various wars that took place, and I have a feeling, based on nothing more than a hunch, that much the same happened in ancient Crete. It is also quite possible that something like this occurred in Egypt, but I have no evidence of this.

I think in Celtic and pre-Celtic times witches had great scope and used their powers wisely and with restraint. In Rome I think they had too much opposition from conflicting sects, from the Roman character, the mixture of the population and, of course, Christianity, which, together with various wars and invasions, put them out of the running for a thousand years.

About the time of the end of the Crusades, however, men's minds began to be rather freer; the shock of the total defeat and destruction of the Crusaders, together with the new ideas these had brought from the East, made men think. And there was a chance that the witches might have had a beneficial effect. But Pope Innocent III saw clearly that this would be to the disadvantage of the Church, which of course it would have been, though I cannot see it as the direct conspiracy against Christ it was said to be. Tolerance had to be avoided at all costs; so the persecution began. There was so much that bigots and Puritans detested, so they wiped witchcraft out.

During the Renaissance witchcraft might have been expected to revive; but at that time, though men's minds had suddenly become freer, they had also turned to Kabbalistic types of magic, and learning had suddenly discovered many new types of poison. All this promised quick and easy effects which you could perform yourself. In England, in Elizabeth's time, there was learning and more freedom of thought; but Italian poisons arrived at the same time, and were used; also there seem to have been many outbreaks of ptomaine poisoning, due to more trade and importation of goods, and the blame was put on the witches. Religious feeling was still high. Neither side had any use for the tolerance that witches preached. After someone made a wax image of her and stuck pins in it, Elizabeth was persuaded that a witch or sorcerer had done it and passed a law against witchcraft and magic. You could be put in the pillory for practising magic, but there were few convictions and many of these may have been plain poisoning. If you killed anyone with a sword, poison or magic, that was murder, a crime against the common law. The Pope had made magic criminal and Bishops took the law more or less into their own hands; but it was not the law of the land. I think that if Elizabeth had had children and they had carried out her policy, we would have had a very different idea of witches and the May Games and their like would still be performed; there might still be a Merry England. But unfortunately she died without issue.

In Scotland, the Earl of Bothwell was thought to have had great powers with, if he was not the actual head of, the Scottish witches, and James believed he was using these powers trying to kill him and gain the throne for himself. Terrible and long-drawn-out tortures produced some confessions and the strong persecution began. The Puritans had their chance and brought the persecution to England. It is said that the Great Rebellion was largely fomented because Charles I objected to people being condemned to death for witchcraft with no evidence, or against all evidence (vide *Four Centuries of Witch Beliefs,* by Mervyn Peake).

Anyhow, the hunt was up again. Anyone likely to be a witch must be exterminated and his children with him.

In spite of it all, witches still linger on. They deliberately never know where the next coven is. If they do not know, they cannot tell, for who knows when the persecution may break out again? But I think we must say good-bye to the witch. The cult is doomed, I am afraid, partly because of modern conditions, housing shortage, the smallness of modern families, and chiefly by education. The modern child is not interested. He knows witches are all bunk—and there is the great fear. I have heard it said: "I'd simply love to bring Diana in, she would adore it and she has the powers, I know; but suppose in some unguarded moment she let it out at school that I was a witch? They would bully and badger her, and the County Council or somebody would come round and take her away from me and send her to an approved school. They do such awful things by these new laws nowadays. . . ." Diana will grow up and have love affairs, is not interested, or is interested but gets married and her husband is not interested, and so the coven dies out or consists of old and dying people.

The other reason is that science has displaced her; good weather reports, good health services, outdoor games, bathing, nudism, the cinema and television have largely replaced what the witch had to give. Free thought or spiritualism, according to your inclinations, have taken away the fear of Hell that she prevented, though nothing yet has replaced her greatest gifts: peace, joy and content.

CHAPTER XII

WHO IS THE DEVIL?

The Gaelic year and the witches' festivals—the God represented by the
High Priest known as the Devil—originally he was a man of learning
or a Druid—the Horned God is replaced by the masked man—how
would the witches recognize the Devil?—they adopt the Church's
slander and adopt Satan to add to their power—discoveries of skull
and crossbones in 18th-century Isle of Man graves and those of earlier
times—was Osiris worshipped there?—similar burials in Yorkshire—
this sign is a symbol of death and resurrection—the uses of girdles as
cords for magical binding—the Queen of Sheba's questions to King
Solomon about occult matters—witch processions took colour from
locality and the superstitions of the day—concealment of the names
of the witch gods.

It is, I think, fairly well known that witches observed four
great festivals: May eve, August eve, November eve (Hallowe'en)
and February eve. These seem to correspond to the divisions of
the ancient Gaelic year by the four fire festivals of Samhaim or
Samhuin (November 1), Brigid (February 1), Bealteine or Beltene
(May 1) and Lugnasadh (August 1). The festivals corresponding
to midwinter and midsummer were both said to have been
founded in honour of female deities: Brigid is a very ancient
goddess of home-crafts and the hearth, Lugnasadh was founded
by Lugaidh in honour of his "nurse" Taillte. Of the witch
festivals, on the other hand, the two summer festivals were in
honour of the goddess, wherein she takes precedence, and the
two winter ones were those wherein the god takes precedence. In
practice it appears to me that in summer the goddess takes
precedence, riding on a broom (or other) stick before the god if he
is present; but in winter he is not superior but merely her equal;
they both ride side by side. It is true, of course, that in summer
the main prayers are to the goddess, while in winter it is chiefly
the god who is prayed to.

Now the god is represented by the high priest (if there is one)
and it is he who was called the Devil in the old days. I was very
curious about him and asked at once when I was "inside", by
which they mean a member of the cult: "Who and what is called

the Devil?" Though members of the cult never use and, indeed, dislike the term, they knew what I meant and said: "You know him, the leader. He is the high priest, the high priestess's husband."

This, though true, was not the exact answer. It really should be: "He is whoever the high priestess appoints to take this position." In practice, she always appoints her husband if he has sufficient rank; but she may appoint anyone who is eligible, including herself; she belts on a sword and acts as a man. In the old days it was often a distinguished visitor who was appointed.

In the times when the People of the Heaths held their meetings the high priest was a man of great learning in the cult, probably a tribal chief, or possibly a Druid, and most likely everyone would know who he was. He was the horned god, received divine honours and possibly took precedence of the high priestess; but when the people of the mixed races became strong in the cult, I think there came a time when the masked (unknown) man took his place, and he was most likely a Norman manorial lord or local churchman who protected the cult in secret. It is very likely that it might be agreed that at one meeting the masked unknown (whom I shall for convenience call the Devil) took the place and, at the next, the old known tribal chief took it. It seems likely that this depended on local arrangements. It was soon found that the uninitiated congregation of farmers, fishermen and such-like had such awe of the great unknown that the cult became more powerful, and that then, even when the old tribal chief played the part, he too was masked and unknown. The Church called him the "devil" and he became known as such.

"If this mysterious man turned up," I asked, "how would you recognize him?" and I found that they had joked about this. They wouldn't know if he were genuine or not! It had never happened to their knowledge; but there was always the possibility of someone from another coven turning up and claiming this right. Actually, the high priestess said: "I'd talk to him and if I found he really had great knowledge and I liked him and found him interesting, I'd treat him as a distinguished visitor and appoint him for the day. Another high priestess might think otherwise." She went on to say: "I wish one of the old sort, a great protector, would turn up, who had a great big house and grounds to lend us for meetings. If he really were of us, I wouldn't bother too much about his vast learning; I'd appoint him and teach him the job." So here's a chance for anyone who wants to play the Devil!

I trust I have made myself clear. The Devil is, or rather was, an invention of the Church. Witches found that the popular view that Satan was one of them added to their power, and rather adopted it, though they never called him by that name except, perhaps, on the rack; and even then, as Dr. Murray has pointed out, sometimes a confession made under torture would name him as their god, but a transcript produced in court would substitute the word DEVIL. Now you cannot blame the poor witch for this. The tortures witches suffered would make anyone confess anything. I have heard that some great man at the time said: "If they did that to me they could make me confess that I'd murdered God the Father and the Son and the Holy Ghost and the Virgin."

Before I finish I would like to mention one or two final matters that may have some bearing on the subject of witchcraft, in the hope that someone can give me more information.

At Rushen Abbey, near Castletown, some curious discoveries have been made (*vide* articles in the *Isle of Man Natural History and Antiquarian Society Proceedings,* March 1935). Mr. W. Christian Cubbon writes (page 111):

"There is another observation worthy of special mention. Its significance has not yet been explained. I refer to the device sometimes found in eighteenth century burials, namely the skull and crossbones. This was found here carried out within the grave itself in actual bone. The isolated heads were found with human thigh-bones crossed under the chins, and one at least of the skeletons had such bones under its chin; this is still to be seen at Rushen Abbey. On discussing this peculiarity it was said to have been observed in Ireland but passed over as being accidental, or having no known significance. With one was also found a bronze figure of the Egyptian god Osiris; Reginald Smith of the British Museum and Sir Arthur Keith pronounce it to be of early or pre-Roman date."

Mr. Cubbon, who excavated them, told me that this figure was found in the grave of the man with thigh-bones under his chin. I have seen this skeleton; the legs are complete and laid out straight, so it was someone else's thigh-bones which were used. I have examined the figure, which is the usual type of Osiris, with a short sword and scourge crossed on his breast—the symbols of death and resurrection I believe. It is fascinating but improbable to think that cult of Osiris could have reached the Isle of Man at this early date, and I would suggest that it has been sold by some unscrupulous pilgrim as the figure of a saint, if it were not for these reasons. The bones were apparently buried in early Norman times and are thought to have been identified as of King Olave and his family who were massacred in 1142. (Probably the heads without bodies had been stuck on posts.) People also suggest that they were pirates and so were buried in this way. But the skull and crossbones was not adopted by pirates until the seventeenth century, in spite of what movies or boys' books say.

Professor Varley of University College, Accra, tells me that he excavated a number of skull-and-crossbones burials at Lissett, East Riding of Yorkshire, during the construction of an airfield there in 1940. This had to be done hastily owing to the war and he found nothing by which he could date them; but personally he believed they were of about the Viking period. He said he sent in all his reports to Mr. Elmer Davis of Cardiff Museum, and he had heard no more about them, so has not published his report.

Professor Varley himself has no idea of the reason for or the meanings of these burials, and was interested to know of their occurring elsewhere.

So we have cases of these burials in Man, Yorkshire and Ireland. People reverence their dead, and do not do such things for fun; it must have had some meaning for them. If it was simply a case of people being beheaded, where did the crossbones come from, and were they their own or someone else's?

It has been suggested that they were cases of cannibalism, the heads being buried and the bodies eaten. But cannibals would not fetch other bones to bury with the heads, and they usually split all the big bones to get the marrow, and these thigh-bones are all intact.

The skull-and-crossbones sign is often found in old tombs and cemeteries; I believe it goes back to Roman times and is the symbol of death and resurrection. When I was made a Mason I was told the skull and crossbones represented "death" and the blazing star "resurrection". Now this star is also a pentacle. As I have said, in old times witches used a skull and crossbones to represent their god when his representative, the high priest, was not present. Nowadays the priestess assumes a position much like that of Osiris to represent the god in his death form, then opens out her arms to represent the pentacle, resurrection. The first gesture also represents a triangle formed by the head and elbows, and the second a five-pointed star (pentacle.) Both triangle and pentacle have special meanings to them. I have already told the story of the Lord of Sidon, and the skull and cross-bones which became a talisman for the Templar Order. Commentators have always supposed that this story came from some spy who saw and misunderstood a ritual which actually took place. Now, although there was much "politics" in the persecution of the Templars, those in charge of the persecutions tried to make the charges plausible. As at this time most churches had skulls and bones of saints which were given divine honours, it is to be presumed that there was something different about the Templar usage. Since paying honours to a skull was common in all churches, did it here represent "Death and Resurrection"? Was it honouring the god of "Death and what lies beyond"? Are there any possible connections between these beliefs and these burials?

Another charge brought against the Templars was that they wore girdles or cords which had some occult meaning. Sometimes it was said that these cords had bound the head which they worshipped. Several writers say that in their girdles lay their idolatry. The Church also accused the Cathari of wearing a cord, implying that there was something wicked in doing so.

The Church therefore at the time accused witches of raising storms, poisoning wells and other serious crimes—and of wearing girdles! Of course, this may have been only a stock charge, brought against everyone; but it seems that it must have meant something to the general public, or it would not have been used in days when every monk and friar and nun wore a rope girdle. Writers, puzzled by these charges, have suggested that these cords were in some way connected with the triple thread that the Indian Brahmins wear; but this is most unlikely at that date.

Now a witch has eight working tools. Of these, five are used only for special purposes; but there are three that she must have in every operation, and cords are among these three. She could at times have worn the cord as a girdle, to disguise it.

J. S. M. Ward in *Who Was Hirim Abif?* quotes the legends of the Jews, which give the twenty-two questions with which Balkis, Queen of Sheba, tested King Solomon's knowledge. These questions are thought to refer to the secret initiation ceremonies of Astarte-Tammuz. Question 9 is peculiar, and clearly refers to things used for ritual or magic.

Sheba: "Which are the three that neither die, nor do they have bread put into them, yet they save lives from death?"

Solomon: "The Staff, the Cord, and the Ring."

The Staff is the "Wand" of the conductor of souls who conducts one through the Underworld. The Cord is the "Cable Tow" with which the candidate is bound, a willing victim properly prepared for sacrifice. The "Ring" symbolizes the "Vesica piscis" of rebirth.

Witches believe that much of their knowledge came from the East and they think there are witch practices described in the Kabbala, notably verses 964–969 of the Greater Holy Assembly of the Book of Zohar and elsewhere. Similar things occurred in most religious cults at the same time, but I think it must have been a Kabbalist who pointed these passages out to them.

Referring to the story the witches told me of their dressing up and riding out to scare people, I mention the following, quoted by Miss Christine Hole. Miss Burne in her *Shropshire Folklore* relates a story told by a little girl who was with her father near War Minsterley when they saw a great company of queerly dressed horsemen. The father apparently knew what it was and made her kneel down and cover her face, saying she would go mad if she did not. But the little girl looked through her fingers and gave a very good description of the leader, a man with a green cloak, a green cap with a white feather and a golden belt with a sword and a hunting horn in his hand. There was also a lady dressed in green, having a white band with a gold ornament on it and a dagger in her belt. Her long golden hair hung loose to her waist. There was a host of others who swept past and left them unharmed.

The old superstition was that Woden was hunting and that no one could look on a god unharmed; he would be killed or blinded at the least. Anyone hearing the wild hunt approaching would therefore fling himself flat, hiding his face in the grass. Little girls do make up stories; but this story rings truer than most. If she had seen such a ride, she would tell it in just this way.

The pity is that no one seems to have asked the father what he saw or what he knew. Of course, she may have been telling as happening to her something that really happened to her great-grandmother. There might have been such a local tradition, and many of the witches were what we called thirty years ago "bright young things", as their sabbats are quite as bad and wild as a hectic cocktail party or an old-time Christmas party, when people were not afraid to enjoy themselves. If these were witches' rides, it is clear why the riders have different names in different places. When all the talk was of the Devil, the leader would dress as Satan; when it was of others, as of Woden, of King Arthur in Somerset, of Sir Walter Calverley in Yorkshire and of Wild Edric in Shropshire, doubtless the leader would also dress the part required.

As I write I am asked: "Why won't the witches let you tell the gods' names? Are they Satan and Beelzebub?" So let me assure you they are not any devils' names. Concealing the gods' names is an ancient practice. Among the Egyptian gods, the real names of Amon and of other gods whose names are sacred are unknown. Referring to the god we call Osiris, Herodotus, who was initiated, says, speaking of the exposure of the sacred cow: "At the season when the Egyptians beat themselves in honour of one of their gods whose name I am unwilling to mention . . ." and: "On this lake it is that the Egyptians represent by night his sufferings whose name I refrain from mentioning." He knew these names; but they were secret.

*   *   *   *   *

CHAPTER XIII

RECAPITULATION

What is the Witch "Power"?—Difficulties about recording witches' rites—
Aleister Crowley uses his own blood—the failure of the experimental
method because witch effects depend upon real feeling—the origin of
the stories about witches turning into animals—a witch's account of a
belief 500 years old—"the gods need our help, we go to their lovely
country at death and are reborn among our people and our sufferings
perfect us"—another account: "something seems to brush against my
soul"—difficulties about the shrill calls and the noisy dances—the
meeting dance—a method of making you fighting mad—witches'
dance was the origin of the waltz through the *Volta*—Dr. Margaret
Murray's account of a picture of a male witch of the 17th century
and his familiar—Robert Graves imagines an ideal government like that
of ancient Crete—the ecstasy of the goddess is reached by various
ways, but regular performance of rites is necessary.
Blood Sacrifice.—Not necessary but may aid materialization—lies about
sacrificed infants invented by the Church to obtain baptism fees.
Sabats.—Possible derivation from Sabazius, but quite probably adapted from
the Christian Sabbath.
Can Witches Make Love Charms?—Advice how to bring the young together.
Is it Possible for Witches to do People Harm?—The use of a battery of human
wills—the tradition of the cursing litanies of the Dominicans, and a
modern induction curse in a Christian Science Church.
Witch Marks.—Meaning appears to lie in certain bracelets and signs, also
perhaps in necklaces.
The Witch's Tools.—Old tools are always better as they have power—enough
to have a witch's knife, censer and cord, etc.—the disguising of tools
—use of incense and anointing oil.
What is the Witch Power?—Essentially mind over matter by the use of
massed human wills, focused upon some part of a person—modern
confirmation of this method by radiesthesia or dowsing, a kind of
natural wireless—the author visits the Gold Coast of Nigeria to trace
links with Voodoo—"there are many paths leading to the centre"—
magic of all kinds attempts to evoke spirits and beliefs in their power
over natural phenomena, using blood, etc.—the witch repudiates these
methods but believes in influencing other minds by long-range
hypnotism—the power of determination—the author defines the
anthropologist's job as investigating people's actions and beliefs, not
moralists' theories—could witchcraft control the hydrogen bomb?

WHAT IS THE WITCH "POWER"?

I FIND I have written twelve chapters; so, this being a book
about witches, I think I must add another to make it up to
thirteen, and to give some final explanations.

First I must make it clear—I am a humble member of a coven. I am not its head or leader in any way, and I have to do what I am told.

People often speak as if I owned a coven and could call it up to perform for them in public. I can and have occasionally introduced people to a witch, when the witch was willing and agreeable. More than this I cannot do.

RITES

I have been asked to photograph their rites. This they usually do not allow—they do not wish to be recognized. The other difficulty is that the places where they work are usually small. The circle takes up the centre, and I could not get far enough away to get my group in, even if they were willing.

Many people say: "We have lived in England all our lives and have never seen a witch, so we don't believe they exist." I can only say: "I have been to Rome many times, but, though I've never had the pleasure of seeing the Pope, I do not doubt that he exists." Many people say: "Witches use blood and all sorts of nasty things in their rites." All I can say is: "I have never seen it done, and my friends say they do not use them." Their writings forbid them to use blood or anything that can cause pain or fright, while admitting that freshly shed blood can give power, the actual words being: "Power flashes forth from newly shed blood, but the use of an animal, for instance, is hateful and cruel."

But a witch friend suggests to me that the use of blood drawn from your own body might be permitted. The late Aleister Crowley used occasionally to perform a ceremony, gashing his breast and using his blood, and it is quite possible some witches do this. All I can say is, I have no knowledge of its being done. The same witch, in answer to a suggestion by a member of the Society for Psychical Research, said:

"I doubt whether performing a series of magical experiments to observe the result for the sake of psychic research would ever work. If people had only a ha'p'orth of *practical experience* they would never make such a proposition, because in successful magical operations one of the strongest stimuli is the *emotional factor*. Before you can do any harm to your enemy by means of a wax image you must be in a genuine and spontaneous rage, as you would need to be before you knocked him down physically.

"Before you can work a love charm you must feel *genuine* and passionate desire for the object of it. These states of mind cannot be switched on and off at will to please the S.P.R. I believe the same thing may apply to astral projection. The records we have of successful projections are nearly always the result of strong and spontaneous desire. The exceptions are the cases of people in feeble health."

This is simply one witch's opinion, but I think it is very generally held. She speaks as if she knows something of how to make a wax image, but she says this is only general knowledge. Up to now I have not found anyone who knows the exact rite used. I have not the slightest doubt that some still know it, though they won't admit it. I particularly want to get it because I think it is apt to be more or less unchanged from the days when the cave man practised it, and knowledge of this might give one some idea of what a cave man thought.

I have asked witches what is the origin of the story of their turning into animals. To them it is only a joke; but they have memories of confused stories that at times they would play sorts of games, much as children do. If they were going across country, for instance, they would say: "Let us go as hares," and try to imitate hares running; or as goats, butting each other, or as deer; and there is a suggestion that in the burning time they were told: "If you see anyone behaving as an animal, they have become an animal. If questioned, say you saw no man, but only a hare, or a goat, etc., because if you simply lied and said you saw no one they might know you lied, but if you said you saw some goats, and believed it, you had the resemblance of truth, even under torture."

Of course there is a very widespread belief in men turning into animals, and the witch's explanation may not be the true one, but it is the only one they know of.

In answer to other questions, one told me this, and I think that this belief must have come down from four to five hundred years past at least:

"In the Christian belief you have a good God, or one who is

good to you, whom you say is all-powerful and who greatly desires worshippers. Yet you must not ask *Him* directly for what you want, but pray to some saint, who is a dead man, as we understand it, though one whom we would call the mighty dead, and you must give money before you can hope to receive favour. But why should an all-powerful God, or your Mighty Ones, be eternally in need of money? *Our* gods are not all-powerful, they *need* our aid. They desire good to us, fertility for man, beast and crops, but they need our help to bring it about; and by our dances and other means they get that help.

"When we die we go to the gods' domain, where having rested a while in their lovely country we are prepared to be born again on this earth; and if we perform the rites correctly, by the grace of the Great Mother we will be reborn among those we loved, and will remember, know and love them again, while those who do evil will have a stern schooling in the gods' domain before they are fit to be reborn again, and then it will be among strangers. Being reborn again we ever progress, but to progress we must learn, and to learn ever means suffering. What we endure here in this life fits us for better in the next, and so we are heartened to endure all the trials and troubles here, for we know that they but help us to higher things. Thus the gods teach us to look forward to the time when we be not men any more, when we become one with the Mighty Ones.

"Ours is a religion of love, pleasure and excitement. Frail human nature needs a little warmth and comfort, to relieve us from the hardness and misery of life and from the cold austerity of the Church's preaching—comfort on earth, not in some far-distant paradise beyond the grave.

"We worship the divine spirit of Creation, which is the Life-Spring of the world and without which the world would perish. To us it is the most sacred and holy mystery, proof that God is within us whose command is: 'Go forth and multiply.' Such rites are done in a holy and reverent way."

Another said: "We ever pick out those who have a little inherent power and teach them, and they practise one with the other and they develop these powers. We only seek to live quietly and worship our gods in our own way and enjoy ourselves in our own fashion and be content and at peace. The art

only comes by developing your own power, and not by the
stroke of a magic wand. It is a strange mystical experience. You
feel a different person, as if much dross were sloughed off. There
is some strange mystery of worship, delicate as a dream. It is as
if I were in a trance during the rites; I can scarcely remember
what happened; something seems to brush against my soul and I
ever think of it with excitement—the old secrets of joy and
terror quicken my blood."

Remember this: you will never advance if your blood is not
stirred and quickened, for truly "the Blood is the Life". The
fact is that the rites do affect many, if not all, of the people in a
curious way, and they usually feel very much better after performing them. This is not merely suggestion, as initiates who
know nothing about it feel just the same.

In the good old days, when if you went half a mile from the
village at night you could be sure no one would spy on you,
because everyone not of the Craft was frightened to be out in
the dark, it was possible to have the old dances, with plenty of
music, to shrill out the calls, to have the chants and to make all
the noise you wanted to. But nowadays you have to work in
small rooms, where you cannot make a noise without the neighbours complaining. The result of this is that the old dances are
being forgotten. The dance in the circle can be kept up, as
long as you dance quietly, but the calls—long shrill cries, which
vibrate and produce terror—cannot be used. The spiral or
meeting dance is sometimes performed if there is room. This
is a sort of "follow my leader" dance, the priestess usually
leading, dancing round in a right-hand spiral to the centre,
when she suddenly turns and unwinds the spiral. As she does
this, she kisses each man she meets and all the other girls do the
same. They say it is called the meeting dance because in the old
days people came from distant parts and did not know each
other, and this was designed to get them acquainted. But one
man told me he had danced it at a church hall when he was a
boy; so it may simply be an old children's game which the
witches have taken over, or vice versa. Nowadays the only music
they can have is a gramophone, or sometimes a sistrum, a rattle,
or a small drum, played softly.

Fifteen years ago I heard many of the old tunes. Unfortunately I know nothing about music and I did not note them down.

They showed me one queer trick with music which I described in my novel *High Magic's Aid*, in the chapter called "Music Magic". They told me they could make me fighting mad; I did not believe it, so they got me to sit, fixed in a chair so that I could not get out. Then one sat in front of me playing a little drum; not a tune, just a steady tom-tom-tom. We were laughing and talking at first . . . it seemed a long time, although I could see the clock and knew it was not. The tom-tom-tom went on and I felt silly; they were watching me and grinning and those grins made me angry. I did realize that the tom-tomming seemed to be a little quicker and my heart seemed to be beating very hard. I felt flushes of heat, I was angry at their silly grins. Suddenly I felt furiously angry and wanted to pull loose out of the chair; I tugged out and would have gone for them, but as soon as I started moving they changed their beat and I was not angry any longer.

I said: "It is just suggestion," but they insisted it was something more—that it was an old secret and could be used to make men fighting mad before a charge. I have read that in Napoleon's army they had drummers to play the *pas de charge* which would make anyone want to fight; and I suppose the Highland war pipes do something of the sort.

Old books speak of a round witch dance in a circle all facing outwards, something like the ladies' position in the first stage of a Paul Jones. No one I have asked has ever seen this. There is indeed a sort of back-to-dance dance, couples linking arms at the elbows, and I have danced it; but I think you have to be very young really to enjoy it. I have also seen a sort of *Volta*, only danced alone, advance three steps and back one, but I have never seen them actually dance it in couples, possibly owing to the smallness of the room and the lack of the proper music. If there were room and space I think it would be a most appropriate dance, and I think what was said three hundred years ago is actually true, viz.: "A new witch dance hath come into France out of Italy, and it is all the rage, everyone is dancing it." Before that time practically all the dances were square dances; I think the *Volta* was the first in which you really held your partner and

that from it the waltz was evolved. At first the waltz was stig-
matized as "that most indecent dance", because you held your
partner all the time.

I found these verses in a witch's book. The owner did not
remember where they were copied from or if they were ancient
or modern, if they were by someone who had seen the dance
or simply by someone with a vivid imagination. So, with acknow-
ledgement to the unknown author and congratulations on a
good bit of description or imagination, I give them:

> Twilight is over, and the noon of night
> Draws to its zenith, as beyond the stream
> Dance the wild witches, fair as a dream
> In a garden, naked in Diana's sight,
> Flaming Censers on the sweet altar, light
> Gleams on the waters, drifting vapours teem,
> Laughter and swaying white shoulders gleam.
> Oh joy and wonder at their lovely sight!

The author of this evidently had no faith in the foul old witch
story.

In Vol. LXIII of *Folk-Lore* for December, 1952, printed
under Collectanea, is an extremely interesting article by Dr.
Margaret Murray, with a reproduction of a picture in the Sheffield
City Art Galleries; and the existence of this picture should, I
think, be better known. I quote what Dr. Murray says about it:

A MALE WITCH AND HIS FAMILIAR

"The modern popular idea that a witch was always a
hideous spiteful old hag is entirely erroneous. There were
almost as many male witches as female; witches sat on the
Councils of Kings and took part in the affairs of state; they
wielded power, often with great ability, and were sometimes
the actual rulers of the realm, the power behind the throne;
they were consulted by the highest in the land in matters of
difficulty whether public or private. In the villages they were
the advisers for all illnesses of mind or body. When Reginald
Scot wrote in 1584 the male witch was so confident of his

high position that he often wore a kind of uniform to distinguish him from ordinary folk. Still earlier, the female witch was decked with black lambskin and white catskin, with polished metal and shining stones.

"Authentic contemporary portraits are extremely rare, though a few are known. The accompanying illustration is from a painting of the 17th century, and portrays a male witch with his familiar. The whole aspect of the man shows that he was used to power, and his garments indicate that he was a person of some wealth. The fierce cat in his arms is clearly content to stay, half-hypnotized by the caresses of these strong and capable hands.

"The picture measures $7\frac{1}{2}$ in. $\times$ $5\frac{1}{2}$ in., and is now exhibited in the City Art Galleries, Sheffield. The flesh is the normal flesh-colour for portraits of the period; the hood is mid-green with antennae and bells; the coat is russet; the background is black. The cat is the true colour for a witch-cat, i.e. fawn-brindle."

As Dr. Murray so forcibly stresses, and as I have endeavoured to tell in this book, witches were a very good and useful class of people. Robert Graves in his novel *Seven Days in New Crete* shows us an ideal world where people daringly experimented in all kinds of government and decided to go back to the type enjoyed by the people of ancient Crete, where they had a king to govern and carry out orders who was however "removed" occasionally, while the whole running of the country was entrusted to witches, who took their responsibilities seriously, no politics being allowed. If the people were bored or wanted a war, they were quite free to have one, but were only permitted to fight in certain areas where they could do no damage, and no weapons except quarter-staffs were permitted to be used; these provided the maximum of fighting and fun with the minimum of expense and damage. I think that this was not altogether written as a joke but rather as an ideal.

It is believed by witches that by acting a part you really take on the nature of the thing you imitate. This is really the basis of the cave-man's magic. By making the clay image of the animal you wish to kill, and by knowing its name, you establish a link between them, so that when he stuck spears into it it gave him power to kill it when he hunted it. That these beliefs may seem rather like children's games to some does not alter the fact that primitive men do behave like this, and so do the witches. By acting the part of the goddess the priestess is thought to be in communion with her; so the priest, acting as the god, becomes at one with him in his aspect of Death, the Consoler, the Comforter, the bringer of a happy after-life and regeneration. The initiate in undergoing the god's experiences becomes a witch.

Witches quite realize that this communion does not occur every time one assumes the goddess position, but they very soon realize that by doing so they begin to receive thrills which are apt to grow more and more intense when the trance comes on. They KNOW! It is no use saying: "This is only suggestion, or the subconscious mind." They reply: "We quite agree; suggestion or the subconscious mind are simply some of the tools which we use to help to open the Door."

As indicated before, I have little doubt that in the old days if a party were setting out for a long journey across rough country they would say: "We will go as hares," or some other animal, and would imitate the animal's movements, thinking that in some mystical way they had taken on that animal's nature. It may have been partly a game; but whatever it was it took their minds off a long and tedious journey, and they doubtless found they could go farther and faster with less conscious effort than if they had walked in the ordinary way. In modern terminology we should say that they had stimulated the unconscious mind.

It is the old case of: "Unless you experience it yourself you will never believe. When you have experienced it, you don't believe, you KNOW."

And, when you have once known the goddess, does anything else really matter? To attain this state there are many roads, and dancing is perhaps the easiest; the calls and chants help, the attitude of the other members is of the greatest assistance—but the true secret is within oneself, and also to some extent in one's partner or assistant in the art, and it is not a thing that can be forced. A quiet knowledge that you will do it, and a steady and regular performance of the rites, are all that is really necessary, although other things help. Short cuts are useful, but you must use them carefully as they are apt to lead you astray and to involve more work in the end. You must first believe it is possible; then, use the method, or preferably a combination of the various methods that may be used together. When you have once attained the ecstasy you know that it exists and may be attained again. You must banish all feelings of *can't*, fix in your mind: "*I can and will*."[1]

There are a number of spiritual powers which many people do not recognize as such, e.g. the various forms of inspiration, music and poetry, clairvoyance and magical awareness; but the greatest of all these is love. All these aids should be employed under instruction, as there are difficulties and dangers in their undiscriminating use.

BLOOD SACRIFICE

The first witches I met denied ever using blood in any way and I think they were speaking the truth according to their lights. I have already quoted them as saying that though freshly shed blood might give some extra power at a critical moment, it would be wrong or sinful to kill an animal for that purpose, and that they would not think of doing it. Indeed at that time I did not myself see how it would fit in with our system of magic. Lately, however, talking it over with someone, he pointed out to me that it was not at all necessary to kill anything; that one could draw blood from his own body and that the late Aleister Crowley, as mentioned above, occasionally performed a rite when he cut his own breast and made use of the blood. Traditionally this aids materialization in ceremonies of evocation. Of course it is well known that in the Great Mystery of Magic the magician is always the victim in a certain sense. Now the people I know have never attempted materialization; but mention of such practices does occur in the rituals, etc. So that these must have been practised in the past, and there are possibly many covens, of which I know nothing, who may use these methods today: that is, use blood to obtain certain results. Of course the old stock charge of killing unbaptized babies is ridiculous; it was only

[1] *See* Note 4 (page 159).

invented to scare people into having their babies baptized and *paying the fees*. It is impossible for large numbers of unbaptized babies to disappear without the police asking questions.

THE SABBATH

I asked my friends what was the real meaning of the Sabbath and they don't know. They know that books say that it is from Sabazius, who was identified with Dionysus and Zeus, also said to be the same as the Jewish Oreb, Lord God of Sabaoth.

Plutarch in *Synus*, Vol. IV, 6, says that the Jews worship Dionysus and that their Sabbath was so named after Sabazius, which was one of his forms. My friends agree that the cult of Dionysus had some connection with their own. This is clear from some of the rituals. They have also read that the first Jews who settled in Rome were expelled under the law which forbade worshippers of Jupiter Sabazius to live in Rome; but they cannot reconcile the Jewish worship with their own. Those who have thought on the matter have a theory that it is simply a word taken from the Christians when Christianity first came to Britain. There would be no resident priests in the "outlands", the witch districts, and services of the revival-meeting type would be held by strolling priests, possibly on Sundays, and the phrase "Sabbath Meetings" would become attached to them. Thus the word Sabbath might be taken by the heathen to mean a religious get-together of a rather loud-singing type. The term "Witches' Sabbath" might easily be applied to their meetings by the Christians themselves in a form of persiflage, adopted as a joke by the witches, in fact. But my friends do not say that this is necessarily gospel truth, it is only their own theory as to how it might have occurred.

CAN WITCHES MAKE LOVE CHARMS?

Witches have many formulae for making all sorts of charms, though few use them nowadays; when stripped of their superstitious practices they chiefly amount to forcing one's will into an object with the aim of influencing the waverer's mind: "Be brave, nothing can harm you, the object of your affection will love you" type of thing. Coupled with this, however, are instructions as to its use, and if you can carry them out I have little doubt that the charm would have some effect. For instance, a charm to make a young couple love each other ends with: "Try to ensure that the pair are thrown together alone, in exciting and if possible dangerous circumstances (or let them think they are dangerous). Soon they will begin to rely on each other; then let them know that a love charm has been made. If they be of the cult, make them perform the rites together and the charm will soon act."

If I were only a quarter of my age, I wish that someone would try that charm on me!

Is it Possible for Witches to Do People Harm?

This is a question I am often asked. I can only say that I have not known them try. I know no spells to this end. But anyone can make a new spell for himself, and the witches' way of training couples to work together, then a number of couples to work so as to form a sort of battery of human wills, is I think a most efficient way of doing things. I believe that it is a historical fact that in the thirteenth century Pope Innocent IV by a bull *Elsi Animarum*, dated November 21, 1284, greatly offended the Dominicans; and it has become a proverb in the Vatican, "A Litaniis Predicatorum, Libera nos Domine", which is translated: "From the litanies of the Dominicans, O Lord, deliver us." This was because the Dominicans had recited a special prayer against the Pope each day after Matins, and he died in less than a month's time. Now one would think that a Pope would not be merely frightened to death by some monk's prayers; it seems to argue some objective validity in the process. I have heard it said before in similar circum tances: "Of course, it is only a coincidence but he is very, very dead!" and many years ago I remember seeing in the papers reports of a curious lawsuit in New York where sworn evidence was produced in court to the effect that a certain unorthodox branch of the Christian Science Church was supposed to meet regularly and after prayers say: "We think of Brother ——, we wish him well, we wish he were in the *best place for him, six feet underground,*" and firmly fix the idea of the Brother as dead or buried in their minds. They were said to have frightened many people to death that way. I believe that finally an injunction against these practices was granted, but I am not sure. So perhaps a witch can do what monks and Christian Scientists can do.

Witch Marks

I have never seen or heard of these among witches. Dr. Murray suggests that there were tattoo marks as a means of recognition. I think it very probable that in the burning times something of the sort was used, but the ones I know have never heard of it except in Dr. Murray's books *Witchcraft in Western Europe* and *The God of the Witches,* in which they are very interested. Witches feel they owe a debt of gratitude to Dr. Murray for being the first to tell them that they were not the poisoners, diabolists or impostors that practically all other writers call them.

The only distinct mark that I know of is that ladies of a certain grade are entitled to wear a bracelet with their name and grade sign engraved on it, and as the uninitiated would not recognize these, they are often worn in public. Another witch would of course recognize them, even at a distance. There is also a higher order, the witch's garter; but this is never worn so that it can be seen in public. I have mentioned a necklace, but this can be of any sort as long as it is fairly conspicuous. They have no story of its origin or meaning; it is merely the custom. Myself, I think that there must be some story to the effect that the goddess always wore a necklace; I believe that Astarte always wore one and was known as the Goddess of the Necklace, being otherwise "sky-clad", as they say in India. I have known one or two witches who wear talismans on their necklaces, but these are mainly astrological, being made for the owner only, and they bear no witch signs, so that I am inclined to think that the necklace itself is the important thing.[1]

[1] *See* Note 5 (page 159)

Necklaces were important things both to Celt and Saxon. Some important priestess must have set the fashion. Thank goodness we are not plagued with people in the cult who are continually changing the fashions. Monsieur Dior would not find any customers for his *New Look*. We are very contented with the *Old Look*.

THE WITCH'S TOOLS

There are no witch's supply stores, so a poor witch usually has to make or improvise her own tools; a novice is often presented with an Athame, and of course in a witch family there are often old tools to be had. Old tools are always preferred, as they are supposed to have *Power*.

If you cannot get these, you are told to attempt to make your own, and I have seen some very clever work. Women are usually helped with making their tools if they have no family ones, but some of them are very clever work-women also.

The tools may be of the simplest construction, but actually, as they are used for a religious purpose, they try to make them as nice as possible.

Of course, the average witch does not have a full battery of tools; not all have the sword, for instance. An Athame (witch's knife), a censer, some cord and one or two other tools are quite enough to work with. For initiations the whole battery of tools has, of course, to be present; but these usually belong to the coven.

It is very amusing to see how clever some witches are in disguising their tools so that they look like something else; indeed, they often are something else, until they are put together in the proper way to be used. For the benefit of anyone interested I am hoping to arrange a small exhibition of witch tools at No. 3 Thackeray Street, Kensington Square, London; also I have a large number which I will be pleased to show anyone at the Museum of Magic and Witchcraft, called locally the Witches' Mill, Castletown, Isle of Man.

Witches use incense in quantities. Nowadays they usually buy this at the nearest church stores, but some compound their own; they are very secretive about this, and I think they put some strong stuff in it; at least I have known people behave rather queerly after it has been burned in a confined space, though it has never had any effect on me—or at least none that I noticed. During the Second World War they had to do without anointing; but nowadays one or two have managed to get small amounts. They keep their source of supply very secret, as, also, what it is compounded with. It smells fine to me, though some people dislike it. It is a powerful smell, and I think that, like the incense, it can have some effect on you if you are suggestible, which I am not; but part of the intention is to cause a shifting of the centres of consciousness. Of this "exstasis", the best English translation is "taking one out of oneself", taking him into communion with the god. But to attain this state lustration is at least advisable; this is in fact the inward as well as an outward cleansing—the old doctrine of penance, cleansing the soul as well as the body; in this way only is the body properly prepared for the goddess to descend and inspire her worshipper. In this way may the trance state be induced, though there are other methods, all to the end of escaping temporarily from the yoke of tradition, to make the soul free; in other words, it gives one something new to live for.

Many people attempt this by drugs, or more crudely by alcohol. But these have extremely bad effects on the body, and any results are at the best often illusions; so seldom make the attempt in that way. In the old days many witches went to the flames laughing and singing; they had a joy of life and of beauty, and the Peace of Death with the promise of return, so they braved the fires, for they believed that they were going to a better world, and they died happy.

WHAT IS THE WITCH POWER?

It is estimated that about nine million people died by torture in one way or another during the persecution, and that quite possibly as many more, chiefly children, died by cold, starvation and exposure as the result of this crusade of persecution. Yet in spite of this extermination some remnants have survived, because people were willing to run the awful risk, and they did so because they believed in the Power.

Now what is this Power? If you ask them they say it is Magic; if you ask them what they mean by Magic, they say they don't know but that it is something that works.

What can this Power be? The easy answer is Mind over Matter. If you believe a thing firmly enough, you will imagine things. While I can believe that Mind has much to do with it, this answer does not satisfy me. Superstition is believing without evidence; science is testing a thing and only believing it when you obtain adequate proof. For this reason science is continually and quite rightly changing its views; they may often confuse cause with effect, as when an early Egyptian scientist noticed that at the coming of the Dog Star the Nile rose, and, to the great benefit of agriculture, was able to predict the annual flooding. That later on it was discerned that the Dog Star did not actually cause the floods, but simply rose at the time of the floods, made no difference to this.

I think that thousands of years ago some medicine men found that by directing the Massed Power of Mind they got good results in hunting. Whether this power affected the animal or the hunter did not matter, it produced results, and they called this Power, Magic. They experimented with this Power and found by rather hit-and-miss methods—superstitious and not proved, if you like—that at times they got results.

One of these superstitions was that there was some connection between part of a thing and the thing itself, so if you could get some of the blood, excrement or hair of a person or animal you could establish a link.

Fifty years ago scientists would have united in saying that this was nonsense, that it was superstition, which it truly is, for there was no proof of it. Nowadays, however, many scientific men believe that living tissues emanate their own radiations in conformity with their cellular structure. A disease affecting these tissues superimposes its own radiations on those of the normal cell; every disease has its own characteristic wave formation, and the patient need not be present; a specimen of blood or saliva is enough. It is said that experiments with special cameras are being made which will record these changes in the cells.

Radiesthesia is a faculty which some people possess of receiving waves or rays and passing them on through muscular reflexes to a divining rod or pendulum. It is what used to be called dowsing when used only to find water, and is probably the force behind table-turning. It is nowadays being investigated by a great number of medical men, priests and research workers generally, because they seem to get results.

It usually begins as almost a childish game: you hide something and the seeker finds it with his pendulum. This was put down at first to telepathy, but many archaeologists found they got good results in discovering things that no living man knew of. That is the scientific test: does it work in enough cases to be of great use? And the verdict seems to be that it does. The rod, pendulum, or whatever you use can do nothing without human contact; it is not one of the forces generally known to science, and mind, will, imagination, belief evidently play big parts. As textbooks say, you need enthusiasm and optimism; if you think it is all rot, or only a child's game, you will at best get childish results.

We all know that wireless works, and this seems a sort of natural wireless. This power has been in use for many years for testing eggs. I believe that dowsers are often used by the police to trace the bodies of missing people. I simply think that this is the force that witches use when they speak of raising Power or Magic. And the great art of using this Power would seem to be to believe firmly that you can do it and to have the fierce determination to make it work.

Now the witch rites and ceremonial are of a nature to fix your mind on the object of the work. Personally, I also believe that they have a great effect in loosening inhibitions and putting you into a favourable state of mind. I think, indeed, that there is something even more than this to be obtained from these methods, but of course that all depends on what you wish to achieve.

Witches were taught that magic was contagious, that what you did to a material object which had formed part of a man's body, or had been in close contact with it, and had absorbed its aura, could have some effect on that person, even at a distance; "forming the link", they called it.

They also believe it is possible to form a mental link without having any material object; but, as Kipling says, that is another story.

Quoting from *Elementary Radiesthesia* by F. A. Archdale, p. 29: "The basis of Medical Radiesthesia is that the pendulum held over a healthy organ gives one reaction, while over an unhealthy one it gives the opposite reaction, which is, we might say, the diagnosis . . . others use samples, such as urine, blood, saliva, etc., taken from the patient, thereby enabling them to carry out their diagnosis at home." P. 35: "There are Radionic Diagnostic Instruments . . . which employ 'samples' from the patient such as a blood spot, lock of hair. . . . A full and thorough diagnosis, or analysis, takes from three to four hours' close concentration, in which time a selection of physical treatment has been made, by finding out a combination of drugs and herbal remedies suited to the discovered condition of the patient."

So we see that Radiesthesia has been brought to the scientific instrument stage. I cannot verify all these claims of course, but I have had a blood spot taken and was given remedies which did me a great deal of good. I am still receiving treatment, the original blood spot being used; it was in London when I was in West Africa, and the treatment still does me good. Many other people have the same experience. It is curious that medical men should believe that there is a connection between the sample of blood taken from me six months ago and that it shows all the changes that have taken place in my body, unless they had considerable previous proof that such things were possible. I am told that Radiesthesia is of great use to veterinary surgeons, as animals cannot tell their symptoms or answer questions. I am not saying that all that is claimed for Radiesthesia is true; all I know is it seemed to do me good, and I think it very curious that while for thousands of years the witch has believed that there was a connection between a body and its severed part, through which a magical link could be established, modern medical men now seem to incline to the same belief. That witches believe it is also possible to link in other ways if they cannot obtain a severed portion of the body, i.e. form a mental link, when they are working solely on the mind, does not affect the matter.

I was much interested in Mr. Pennethorne Hughes's theory,

vide page 23 of his book, that magic was evolved by the Egyptian priests, that one branch of this knowledge came to Europe, becoming witchcraft, the other going to West Africa and thence to America, becoming Voodoo. I know that Frazer and others have mentioned the resemblance between the African cults of the Divine King and Egyptian myths, and I had already noted the resemblance between certain Voodoo practices and European witchcraft; but it seemed to me that the proof of Mr. Hughes's theory must lie in West Africa. If the witches or witch doctors there had the knowledge, they might have passed it on to America.

So I went to the Gold Coast and Nigeria for the winters of 1952 and again in 1953. Now it is extremely difficult to get into real magical circles anywhere. The first year I had no luck; but after I had given a suitably watered-down lecture on witchcraft at Accra, Gold Coast, in January 1954, in (of all places) a Y.M.C.A. building, followed by a small wireless talk, information began to trickle in, and now I have seen magic worked in the Coast fashion. Of course I quite realize they don't tell me all their secrets; from what I have seen they do use two of the processes that witches use to gain power, but these two processes seem to be world-wide.

A European witch is taught "there are many *paths or ways all leading to the centre*", and uses many (or all) of them combined in one operation to gain all the power she can. But, nowadays at least, she is at best an amateur, only practising occasionally, while the African is a professional. Perhaps he finds he can do all he wants by his methods, and so does not need the extra aids the European witch uses. And it is quite possible that they know and use all the witch-methods occasionally. There is a great language difficulty, also there was no reason why they should show me their innermost secrets; but I could find only two resemblances. As the Magic was only done to show me, I cannot say whether it works or not; they assure me, however, that it does. And I asked where the power came from and was told it was from the local gods. They, at least, seemed to have no idea that it came from Egypt.

Now there is abundant evidence of intercourse between Egypt and the Coast; but as far as I can ascertain there is only proof of this *via* Arab caravans during the last thousand years; that is, during the time when they were established native states. It is quite possible that there were established native states of which we know nothing, and that they may have had some communications with Egypt by sea through the Carthaginians and others; but there is no proof of this. So the only communications of which we are certain were at a date when the Egyptian priests had been put out of action first by Christians and afterwards by Mohammedans nearly a thousand years before.

If I only knew exactly what was the system of magic practised by the Egyptian priests, it would be easy to say. That which is described in books has no resemblance to the witches' practices; but it is most likely they had some secret system which they did not mention in their inscriptions.

All I can definitely say is that there are some resemblances between European magic and that used today on the West Coast. Obviously this is not conclusive proof.

Europeans have been going to this Coast in large numbers during the last 500 years and introducing all sorts of beliefs and customs. As an instance, in the year 1485 a Portuguese Don Alfonso d'Aleiro was living up-country in Benin City. He is credited with having introduced guns and coconuts (intentionally) and the practice of crucifixion (unintentionally), through the crucifixes that he and his followers wore. The famous crucifixion tree in Benin City was in constant use until it was destroyed by a British Expedition in 1897. Now, during the period 1400 to 1700 the witch persecutions were raging, so is it not most likely that some poor witch would volunteer for a dangerous and unhealthy exploring expedition to escape the Inquisition? A number of the Kings of Benin were noted magicians and astrologers. They might easily have protected a fellow-worker and picked his or her brains; so, while I am very much interested in Mr. Hughes's theory and would like to know that it was true, I can only say that as far as I am concerned it is "NOT PROVEN".

To recapitulate, Ritualistic Magic, Kabalistic Magic, Art Magic or Black Magic are alike attempting to evoke genii, demons or elemental spirits and forcing or bribing them to cause events to occur, the practitioner believing that such spirits have the power to alter nature, to cause storms, floods or earthquakes for instance. They often use blood, skulls and other nasty things for this purpose. The witch dislikes these methods and thinks her ways are best. True, in the past there have been many cases of sorcerers employing witches; but this was as mediums when something of a spiritualistic nature was attempted, that is, trying to communicate with the spirits of departed human beings who were willing to communicate, and were neither bribed nor threatened.

The witch generally does not believe it is possible to alter nature—to cause storms, for instance; but she does believe that most important events are controlled by some human mind or minds, and that it is often possible to form a link with, and so influence, the minds of others (human or animal) by a means I can only describe as a sort of long-range hypnotism, the results depending on the amount of power raised, the skill in directing it, the sensitivity or otherwise of the brains at the other end and whether they are opposed to the idea which comes into their minds or not; and that their minds may still be so influenced, even if some strong counter-influence is exerted.

Now it is perfectly possible to influence people's minds in great numbers in order to gain your own ends. John Wesley, Gladstone and Hitler all did it on a large scale. None of them changed the minds of all the people they contacted; but the influence was sufficient to change the history of the world, and it was not done by reasoning with people. They simply put an idea into people's minds and rammed it home. All politicians do or attempt to do it. Witches use a different technique to do the same thing. They do not succeed in all their operations and it is difficult for me to assess exactly how many of their successes may have been due to chance; but they do seem to have had a remarkable number of successes. People tell me: "This is easy; either they succeed or they don't, so they have a 50 per cent chance of success", quoting: "If you toss 100 pennies in the air, about 50 per cent will come down heads." But it's not so easy as all that.

As the witch told the psychical research man: "To do magic you must work yourself into a frenzy; the more intense you feel, the more chance of success." You simply can't get the required number of people to do it just for fun, or if it's likely to come off naturally; the chances are then usually 80-90 per cent against.

Other people tell me: "If you are determined enough you can force anything through without having to resort to witchcraft," quoting: "Napoleon said 'There is no such word as *impossible* in the French language,'" but as a witch said when they told her this: "I suppose Napoleon said it in Corsican when we put it into his brain it is *impossible* to cross the English Channel."

Now I have seen things I'm forbidden to talk about, and quite admittedly I'm superstitious because of what I have seen of witches' powers. Also it is easy to see where this superstition could lead to and I know I'm going to be laughed at. I can take it.

As I have said before, an anthropologist's job is to investigate what people do and what they believe, not what moralists say they should do and believe. They may draw their own conclusions and give out any theory, provided they state clearly that these are their own theories, and not proven facts.

I have told you before how the witches performed certain rites and believe they succeeded in influencing the minds of people who controlled the invasion barges.

It is purely my own *theory*, and admittedly founded on *superstition*, but I think they could perform similar rites to influence the brains of those who may control the *Hydrogen Bomb*.

Having said all I am permitted to say, I must now finish. I hope that this book will have been of interest to you, the reader, and as the witches say to each other—

BLESSED BE

NOTES

(1) I remember as a boy reading in the papers of a woman being slowly roasted to death in Ireland as a witch. For an account of this see *Folk-lore*, Vol. 6, 1895: "The Witch-burning at Clonmel".

(2) There was a Celtic custom of binding corpses; the cord with which one had been bound was of great assistance in obtaining second sight. But in the Ancient World there seems to have been a widespread idea that a living person must be bound to enter the presence of the Lords of Death. Tacitus, in *Germania* xxix, tells of sacred groves where men assemble to obtain ancestral auguries, to enter these dominions sacred to the Lords of Death. "All are bound with fetters to show that they are in the power of the Divinity, and if they chance to fall they are not helped to rise. Prone as they are, they must roll along the ground as best they may." This latter shows they were closely bound, as they could not rise themselves; so clearly it was no "token" binding.

Lucian, in his *Vera Historia*, which, though a novel, treats of popular beliefs, tells of living people landing on the Island of the Blessed being instantly bound with chains and brought before the King of the Dead.

The idea of living people, or the newly dead, being thus bound with chains as soon as they went to the land of death may I think be the origin of the old idea that ghosts rattled chains; newly out of Limbo they would still be thus bound.

(3) The gods were as much in need of worshippers as the worshippers were of the gods. Their reproductive energies had to be recruited, so men had to sacrifice to them what was most manly in man and the most womanly in woman.

(4) Iamblichus, in his *Mysteries*, says: "If one knows how, he can set in motion mysterious forces that are capable of contacting the will of another, directing his emotions as the operator desires; this may be done by the spoken word. Ceremonies properly performed, or which proceed from an object properly charged with the power, we call magical."

(5) Diana of Ephesus wore a necklace of acorns; many Celtic goddesses are mentioned as wearing them. At witch meetings every woman must wear one. When the ritual objects are being set out for a meeting, a number of strings of beads are put handy, so that if any witch hasn't brought a necklace, she promptly borrows one for the occasion. I remember one girl coming wearing a small string of pearls being told: "You know, dear, you mustn't do that; get a proper one from the box, one that can be seen." They cannot give me any other reason than that a witch must wear a necklace that is obvious.

A STARTING POINT: GERALD GARDNER'S LIFE AND WORK

BY RONALD HUTTON

GERALD BROSSEAU GARDNER was born on 13 June 1884 at Great Crosby, one of the most prosperous suburbs of the city of Liverpool. His parents were William Robert Gardner and Louise Barguelew Ennis, who lived off the proceeds of a very successful family timber business based in the city; Gerald was their third son out of four. This background was important to him mainly because when both mother and father died in the 1920s, he inherited a substantial private income. He was also proud of his father's social status as a magistrate and his mother's literary interests as a champion of the idea that Francis Bacon had written Shakespeare's plays.

Otherwise the link between him and his parents was a fragile one. He was a sickly child, with chronic asthma, and was handed over to a nursemaid, a domineering lady called Josephine McCombie ("Com"), who beat and neglected him. In his memoirs he never named his parents at all, treating Com instead as the major figure of his childhood.

Nobody seems to have paid any attention to his education, and he taught himself to read and write. The results of this self-schooling remained apparent for the rest of his life in his huge appetite for knowledge, especially of history, folklore, and archaeology, his independence of mind and haphazard way of collecting information, and his eccentric spelling that was often based on phonetic equivalents to words. In 1900, Com married a tea planter in Ceylon and took the adolescent Gerald out there with her as if he were her own child. He remained in the Far East for the whole of his working life.

Until 1908, this was in Ceylon, working successively for two tea plantations, then managing one of rubber trees. Between 1908 and 1923, he acted as manager for rubber plantations in North Borneo and Malaya. The crash in the price of the product drove him to become instead a government inspector of plantations in the southern part of the Malay peninsula, and he was later promoted to principal customs officer of the state of Johore.

During one of his rare visits to England—he came to receive his portion of his father's estate—he met a nurse called Dorothea ("Donna") Frances Rosedale. After a whirlwind romance, they married in London on 16 August 1927, and she accompanied him back to Malaya.

Gardner's memoirs of his many years in Asia depict a hardy, lonely, temperate, and self-contained man, distinguished by three traits. One was his conversion to naturism after nude sunbathing seemed to cure him of a crippling illness. Another was his interest in the past, which resulted in his becoming a pioneer of Malayan archaeology and numismatics, and a collector of Malay weapons. His publications do not now seem to be valued by experts in those fields, but his enthusiasm and his patience in amassing data deserve respect. The third unusual trait was his interest in esoteric religion. Having been brought up in no faith, he took a keen interest in Freemasonry, Buddhism, Spiritualism, and tribal beliefs and practices. From these, he gained a love of ritual and a belief in reincarnation and in the reality of a spirit world.

In 1936, at the age of fifty-two, he was able to take early retirement, his state pension being augmented by his inheritance. His own inclination was to remain in the East, but Donna persuaded him to return to England. In doing so, she unwittingly launched him into becoming one of the handful of people who have changed world history by their retirement hobbies.

The immediate effect of Gerald's release from work was to plunge him into a whirl of new activity: Between 1936 and 1939, he visited archaeological sites in the Near East and joined the national Folklore Society, the Druid Order, and the Co-Masons. In 1938, he and Donna rented a house in Highcliffe, a plush and conservative suburb of Bournemouth, and he became involved with an esoteric society, the Fellowship of Crotona, at nearby Christchurch. It was through this that he claimed to have met members of a surviving coven of pagan witches led by a local lady, Dorothy Clutterbuck, and so discovered Wicca.

No independent evidence has ever been found that he met any such coven—or indeed, that one ever existed—but two things are certain. One is that his interest in ancient paganism, witchcraft, and reincarnation sharpened sufficiently for him to publish a novel, *A Goddess Arrives* (1939), that treated all these themes. The other is that he met in the Fellowship a keen actress and ritualist (a member of the Co-Masons, Crotona Fellowship, and Rosicrucian Theatre), who called herself Dafo. His marriage was happy and stable, but Donna showed no interest in his intellectual and spiritual pursuits; in Dafo he found a companion for both.

With the outbreak of war, he served as an air-raid patrol warden and, from 1944 to 1945, served as co-president of the Bournemouth Historical Association, campaigning unsuccessfully with Dafo to establish a museum of local history.

With the end of the war, Gerald rented an apartment in Ridgmount Gardens, London, and his pursuits became more concentrated on occultism. In 1946, he was elected to the council of the Druid Order, a body practicing a form of philosophical Freemasonry that was regarded as perfectly respectable in Britain. At the same time, however, he and Dafo bought a patch of woodland at Bricket Wood, Hertfordshire, on which to install a replica witch's cottage, apparently as a site for rituals. In 1947, he visited Britain's most famous magician, Aleister Crowley, and undertook the work of reviving the latter's society, the Ordo Templi Orientis, in Britain.

By the following year Gerald had given up this project and instead completed a novel set in the middle ages, *High Magic's Aid*, in which the religion of Wicca features prominently; this is the latest possible date at which that religion might have been developed. The novel was published in 1949, and within a year (at the latest), he was running a Wiccan coven at Bricket Wood with Dafo. In 1950 also, he began to spread word among London occultists of the existence of Wiccans, and in 1951, he commenced a campaign to draw attention to it in the mass media.

Wicca dominated the remaining period of his life. It provided Gerald with a home, in that in 1951 he became associated with the first Museum of Witchcraft in the British Isles, at Castletown in the Isle of Man and, in 1954, bought the premises and made them his principal residence. It provided him with a rapidly growing number of initiates. The most influential was Doreen Valiente, initiated in 1953, who used her considerable talents as a poet and ritualist to develop the Wiccan liturgy, but he constantly encouraged all new initiates to augment the body of texts and assisted the work himself. His marriage was childless, and it is hard to escape the conclusion that his priestesses provided him with surrogate daughters, especially after Donna died in 1960.

He spoke regularly to newspapers and on radio and television, lectured at University College Accra, in what became Ghana, and published three more books. Two of these were expositions of Wicca, *Witchcraft Today* (1954) and *The Meaning of Witchcraft* (1959), while a ghosted autobiography, *Gerald Gardner: Witch*, written by Idries Shah under the name of Jack Bracelin, appeared in 1960. In these works, he paid relatively little attention to the theology of his religion, preferring instead to emphasize its poetry and experiential excitement, and (above all) to relate it to a range of ancient prototypes, from Graeco-Roman mystery cults to northern tribal traditions. He was claiming the whole inheritance of pagan antiquity for it.

Until the 1950s, Gerald impressed observers with his fit, tanned, tatooed body, piercing stare, and abounding energy. Thereafter he grew more frail, and frequently unwell, and he died from a cerebral hemorrhage on 12 February 1964, while on a Mediterranean cruise. He was buried in a public cemetery at the nearest port, Tunis. His friends were left to mourn a person of undoubted charm, kindness, and gentility, an excellent raconteur with a love of jokes and a zest for life. He also had a taste for mischief and at times for duplicity; for example, at least twice he encouraged women whom he had himself initiated into Wicca to pass themselves off to outsiders as members of long-established witch families. His part in the creation of Wicca remains uncertain and deeply controversial. Some have asserted that he developed the whole religion himself, while others still believe his story about encountering one of the last surviving groups practicing an ancient tradition; there are also various theories that fall between those positions. The lack of any clear evidence to substantiate any of them leaves the matter unsettled, and it may always remain so, but there is no doubt that he was the first publicist and propagator of Wicca.

By the time of his death, he had founded a network of covens that spanned the British Isles and had reached America. All the modern branches of Wicca are either based on or influenced by his work. It is the only complete religion (as opposed to sect or denomination) that England has ever given the world. Whether or not Gerald was its parent, he certainly delivered it to humanity.

LOOKING BACKWARD: GARDNER'S SOURCES

BY JUDY HARROW

GERALD GARDNER'S life was extraordinary in many ways. Most important of these, in my opinion, is that, from childhood through early middle age, he lived mostly abroad. He didn't just visit fascinating and exotic places; he made his first two careers—planter, and customs official—in Southeast Asia. During those years, his open-minded and curious nature took him far beyond staid British colonial society, into the homes and even the religious ceremonies of indigenous people, from whom he learned a great deal. This close contact with people who were practicing a living Pagan religion was the best possible preparation for his ultimate career as priest and teacher of Witchcraft.

Reading can never replace experience, but it can help us understand our experiences and put them in context. Gardner was an avid reader and a self-educated scholar who earned the respect of his better-credentialed colleagues in the fields of anthropology and archeology. Later, at his Museum of Magic and Witchcraft on the Isle of Man, he gathered a fine reference library, which is now held in a private collection in Canada.

Only a very few of us can travel as Gardner did, let alone live abroad for years. Even those few will not find what Gardner found among indigenous people living a traditional lifestyle and practicing their tribal religion. Since the Second World War, Western industrialism has inundated formerly remote places, including Ceylon, Borneo, and Malaya, bringing cataclysmic change to ancient lifeways and even to the land itself.

Although we cannot share Gardner's direct experience, some of us will want to explore his reading, the informational context within which he made sense of what he heard, saw, and did. However, although he mentions forty authors and/or books in *Witchcraft Today*, he only rarely provides the kind of full, formal citation that a student who wants to read a book can use to find it. I have attempted to gather and reconstruct as much of this information as I could.

Often Gardner mentioned an author but no title. In such cases, I have given you the titles of books those authors wrote before the publication of *Witchcraft Today* in 1954, and on relevant subjects. Since these are guesses (reasonable ones, I hope), I thought it was important also to note which of these books are in the Gardner Collection because we can at least be sure that he owned them.

Also, since 1954 was a long time ago, I checked which of Gardner's sources have been more recently reprinted, and which are still in print. Happily, more were than I would have guessed. The reprints will be much easier to find. The chart below will also tell you where in *Witchcraft Today* each work is mentioned so that you can see how each one contributed to the Gardner's new synthesis, which was to become the strong foundation of contemporary Witchcraft.

Author	Title	Original Pub. Data	Reprint Pub. Data	Page Cit.	GBG Coll.	In Print
anon.	*Chronicle of St. Denis*	unable to locate		72	no	n/a
anon.	*"Chronicle of Cyprus"*	see Comments, 1		72	no	n/a
anon.	*Key of Solomon*	see Comments, 2		94, 112, 121	yes	n/a
anon.	*Mabinogion* [Welsh classic, widely available in several translations]	see Comments, 3		74, 79	no	yes
anon.	*"Merlin MS."*	see Comments, 4		80	no	n/a
Archdale, Fulbert Audley	*Elementary Radiesthesia and the Use of the Pendulum*	Bournemouth: author, 1950	Pomeroy, WA: Health Research, 1996 0-7873-0039-X	154	no	yes
Atwood, Mary Anne (1817–1910)	*A Suggestive Inquiry into the Hermetic Mystery*	Belfast: Tait, 1920	Kila, MT: Kessinger, 1999 0-7661-0811-2	92	no	yes
Brend, William A. (1873– ?)	*Sacrifice to Attis: A Study of Sex and Civilisation*	London: W. Heinemann, 1936	New York: Gordon, 1973 0-8490-0985-5	96	no	yes
Burne, Charlotte Sophia, ed. (1850–1923)	*Shropshire Folklore: A Sheaf of Gleanings*	London: Trubner, 1883	Wakefield: E.P. Publishing, 1973	135	no	no
Carmichael, Alexander (1832–1912)	*Carmina Gadelica,* see Comments, 5	Edinburgh: Norman MacLeod, 1900	Hudson, NY: Lindisfarne Books, 1992 0-940262-50-9	25	no	yes

AUTHOR	TITLE	ORIGINAL PUB. DATA	REPRINT PUB. DATA	PAGE CIT.	GBG COLL.	IN PRINT
Carus, Paul (1852–1919)	The History of the Devil and the Idea of Evil, from the Earliest Times to the Present Day	Chicago: Open Court, 1900	Chicago: Open Court, 1988 0-87548-307-0	106	yes	yes
Christian, Paul	History and Practice of Magic, James Kirkup and John Shaw, trans.	London: Forge Press, 1952	Kila, MT: Kessinger, 1994 1-56450-471-8	13	no	yes
Craine, David	The Dungeon of St. Germain's: Sidelights of Church Discipline 1600–1800	Isle of Man: Natural History and Antiquarian Society, 1948		50	yes	no
Crowley, Aleister (1875–1947)	12 titles in Gardner Coll., see Comments, 6			47, 138, 146,		
Cubborn, William	see Comments, 7			132	yes	no
Davies, Reginald Trevor	Four Centuries of Witch Beliefs, with Special Reference to the Great Rebellion	London: Methuen,1947	Manchester, NH: Ayer, 1972 0-405-08437-4	17	yes	yes
Evans, Sebastian (trans.) (1830–1909)	The High History of the Holy Grail		Cambridge: James Clarke, 1969 LC 74171444	71, 77–79	no	no
Frazer, James George, Sir (1854–1941)	The Golden Bough	New York: Macmillan, 1922	NY: Oxford University Press, 1998 0-19-283541-6	155	no	yes
Goethe, Johann Wolfgang von (1749–1832)	Faust [literary classic, widely available]			49		yes
Graves, Robert (1895–1985)	Watch the North Wind Rise, see Comments, 8	New York: Creative Age, 1949		144	no	no
Hole, Christina	no title specified, see Comments, 9			17, 135		n/a
Pope Honorius III (d. 1227)	Grimoire du pape Honorius: avec un recueil des plus rares secrets; also typed ms. in Gardner Coll.	1670	Paris: Diffusion scientifique, 1978	113	yes (typed ms.)	n/a

Author	Title	Original Pub. Data	Reprint Pub. Data	Page Cit.	GBG Coll.	In Print
Hughes, Pennethorne	*Witchcraft*	London: Longmans, Green, 1952	Baltimore: Penguin, 1965	17, 22, 33, 93, 98, 102–104, 110	yes	no
Huxley, Aldous (1894–1963)	*The Devils of Loudun*	New York: Harper, 1952	New York: Carroll & Graf, 1996 0-7867-0368-7	108–10	no	yes
"Dean Inge"	unable to locate, see Comments, 10			96	no	n/a
Jennings, Hargrave (1817–1890)	no title specified, see Comments, 11			47		n/a
Jung, Carl Gustav (1875–1961)	many titles, widely available, see Comments, 12			96		
Kipling, Rudyard (1865–1936)	no title specified [Kipling was a major writer of poetry and fiction, often exploring Pagan themes, widely available.]			47	no	n/a
Kramer, Heinrich and James Sprenger	*Malleus Maleficarum,* Montague Summers, trans., see Comments, 13	London: John Rodker, 1928	Magnolia, MA: Peter Smith, 990 0-8446-0169-1	106	yes	yes
Macchioro, Vittorio (1880– ?)	*La Villa dei misteri in Pompeii*	Napoli: Richter, [betw. 1911 & 1925]		82–88	no	no
Marlowe, Christopher (1564–1593)	*Dr. Faustus* [literary classic, widely available]			49	no	n/a
Murray, Margaret A. (1863–1963)	see Comments, 14			17, 99, 132, 143–44, 149	no	n/a
Peake, Mervyn (1911–1968)	*Four Centuries of Witch Beliefs,* see Davies, Hole, and Comments, 15			128	no	n/a

Author	Title	Original Pub. Data	Reprint Pub. Data	Page Cit.	GBG Coll.	In Print
Runeberg, Arne (1912–1979)	Witches, Demons and Fertility Magic: Analysis of Their Significance and Mutual Relations in West-European Folk Religion	Helsingfors: Societas Scientarum Fennica, 1947 (Commentationes Humanarum Litterarum XIV, 4)	Norwood, PA: Norwood Editions, 1974	36	no	no
Spence, Lewis (1874–1955)	An Encyclopedia of Occultism, see Comments, 16	New York: Dodd, Mead, 1920	Secaucus, NJ: Citadel, 1993 0-8065-1401-9	89	yes	yes
Summers, Montague (1880–1948)	see Kramer and Comments, 17			17, 22	yes	yes
Ward, John Sebastian Marlow (1885– ?)	The Hung Society	London: Baskerville, 1925	New York: AMS Press, 1973 0-404-11220-X	71	yes	yes
Ward, John Sebastian Marlow	Who Was Hiram Abiff?	London: Baskerville, 1925	Kila, MT: Kessinger, 1998 0-7661-0451-6	135	yes	yes
Wilson, Bishop	notebook (11/29/1720) [unable to locate]			49	no	n/a
Wolfram von Eschenbach (12th cent.)	The Story of Parzival and the Graal, as related by Wolfram von Eschenbach; interpreted and discussed by Margaret Fitzgerald Richey	Oxford: R. Blackwell, 1935	[edited and translated by Andre Lefevere] New York: Continuum, 1991 0-8264-0346-8	78	no	yes

COMMENTS ON GARDNER'S SOURCES

1. The "*Chronicle of Cyprus*" might be Machairas, Leontios, *Recital concerning the sweet land of Cyprus, entitled 'Chronicle,'* NY: AMS Press, 1980 (reprint of Oxford: Clarendon, 1932). Translated from the Venice manuscript Class VII, cod XVL in the Libreria Nazionale.

2. The *Key of Solomon* is one of the classic texts of ceremonial magic. There are many different translations and versions of it in the

Gardner Collection. Probably the most widely used and widely available of these is Mathers, S. Liddell MacGregor, trans. & ed., *The Key of Solomon the King (Clavicula Salomonis)*, London: G. Redway, 1888 (reprinted by Samuel Weiser in 1989). Mathers was one of the founders of the Golden Dawn, a ceremonial magic order of the late nineteenth and early twentieth centuries that was one of the antecedents of contemporary Wicca.

3. Lady Brigantia, a native speaker of Welsh, recommends the translation by Gwyn Jones and Thomas Jones (London: Everyman, 1949; reprinted 1994, ISBN 0-460-87297-4).

4. The "*Merlin* MS." might be *Merlin; or The Early History of King Arthur: a prose romance* (c. 1450–60) edited by Henry B. Wheatley from the unique manuscript in the Cambridge Library, originally issued as nos. 10, 21, 36, and 112 of the Early English Text Society Originals series (1899), reprinted Millwood, NY: Kraus Reprints, 1987.

5. The Yule chant given on p. 25 appears to be based on a prayer in the *Carmina Gadelica*. See "God of the Moon" on p. 173 of the Lindisfarne Press edition.

6. The extent of Crowley's influence on Gardner has been a subject of continuous and heated debate in our community. Dr. Ronald Hutton's *Triumph of the Moon* (Oxford: Oxford University Press, 2000) contains a thorough review of the issues involved. We know for sure that the two men met when Crowley was very old and in his final illness. Crowley granted Gardner a charter to lead a lodge of his organization, the Ordo Templi Orientis. And there are twelve books by Crowley in the Gardner Collection, more than by any other author. So the influence must have been considerable at one point.

Nevertheless, Gardner never did actually found that O.T.O. lodge. More important, those who trace our roots to him follow a very different core ethic than that taught by Crowley. The Wiccan Rede, as we call it, says, "*An it harm none,* do what ye will," while Crowley's Law of Thelema says, "Do what ye will shall be *the whole of the Law.*" Despite the superficial similarity, these two "prime directives" point in utterly different directions. As might be expected, the two movements have developed very differently since both their founders died, regardless of any friendship or collaboration between the two men.

7. Although Gardner does not specify a book title by Wil-

liam Cubborn, the Gardner Collection includes his *Island History: Dealing with Some Phases of Manx History* (Manchester: Faulkner, 1952).

8. One of Graves's other books, *The White Goddess*, has been profoundly influential among contemporary Witches and neo-Pagans. *The White Goddess* was reprinted by Noonday Press in 1997.

9. Gardner does not specify a title by Christina Hole, a prolific writer on English folklore. The one of her books that seems most relevant is *Witchcraft in England: Some Episodes in the History of English Witchcraft* (London: B.T. Batsford, 1945; reprinted Totowa, NJ: Rowman & Littlefield, 1977). Note: This book was illustrated by Mervyn Peake.

10. "Dean" is an ecclesiastical title rather than a given name. Gardner probably meant William Ralph Inge (1860–1954), dean of St. Paul's Cathedral, who wrote several books on theology and mysticism.

11. Although Gardner does not specify a title for Hargrave Jennings, the Gardner Collection includes *The Rosicrucians: Their Rites and Mysteries* (London: George Routledge & Sons, [after 1887]).

12. Jung was one of the founders of contemporary psychology and the one most sensitive to spiritual issues. His theory of *archetypes* gave us an important new way to understand how the Gods manifest in our daily lives.

13. The *Malleus Maleficarum* is nothing less than the operations manual for the Inquisition, the *Mein Kampf* of its century.

14. Dr. Margaret Alice Murray, who wrote the introduction to the book in your hands, was probably Gardner's most important precursor. She believed that Witchcraft was the vestigial survival of indigenous European religion and that the Witch persecutions of the 15th–18th centuries (the "burning times") were the Church's attempt to wipe out the last remnant of the Old Religion it had supplanted. Murray's conjectures have since been refuted. For a discussion of that scholarly controversy and other related issues, see Margot Adler's book *Drawing Down the Moon* (Boston: Beacon, 1986, pp. 45–66). Still, Murray and her ideas have themselves become an important part of our history because of their influence, which has far exceeded their accuracy.

Murray's 1929 Witchcraft entry for the *Encyclopedia Britannica* (included in reprints until 1969) obviously had a profound influence on popular notions of Witchcraft, opening the way for a climate of tolerance and eventual acceptance. Furthermore, some people were intrigued enough by her suggestions to begin study and experimentation, paving the way for Gardner's creative synthesis.

Murray was primarily an Egyptologist. The three of her books that are pertinent to Witchcraft are *The Divine King of England: A Study in Anthropology* (NY: AMS Press, n.d.), in print; *The God of the Witches* (New York: Oxford University Press, 1992), in print; and *The Witch-Cult in Western Europe* (New York: Oxford University Press, 1971), out of print.

15. Mervyn Peake did not write a book called *Four Centuries of Witch Beliefs*. Reginald Trevor Davies, whom Gardner mentions without specifying a title, did. What Peake did was to illustrate Christina Hole's book *Witchcraft in England*. See comment number 9, on the previous page.

16. Lewis Spence was a very prolific occult writer of his time. Besides his *Encyclopedia of Occultism*, he wrote several other books that might have shaped Gardner's view of Witchcraft, such as *British Fairy Origins* (London: Watts, 1946; reprinted Folcroft, PA: Folcroft Library Editions, 1979), in Gardner Collection; *The Fairy Tradition in Britain* (London: Rider, 1948; reprinted Kila, MT: Kessinger, 1995), in Gardner Collection; *The Magic Arts in Celtic Britain* (London: Rider, 1945; reprinted Mineola, NY: Dover, 1999); and *Myth and Ritual in Dance, Game and Rhyme* (London: Watts, 1947), in Gardner Collection.

17. Montague Summers was a bitter religious fanatic with an irrational fear and hatred of Witchcraft, which he spewed forth in several books. He also did the standard translation of the evil *Malleus Maleficarum*. See comment number 13, on the previous page.

WICCA HERE AND NOW: THE VIEW FROM AN INTERNET CENTER

BY WREN WALKER

"IT IS a strange mystical experience," Gerald Gardner wrote in *Witchcraft Today*. In the years and decades since 1954, when this book was first published, an oftentimes convoluted path has led us to the current explosion of interest in Wicca—and he has proven to be prophetic. Wicca, for better and for worse, has become a household word. Just about everyone knows of someone who is "into that stuff."

The religion of Wicca is today both very much the same and very different from the "Wica" that Gardner portrayed. Some Traditional covens continue to pass along the oath-bound materials and maintain Gardner's original ritual structures. Others, who also identify themselves as Wiccans, have created entirely new modes of worship and celebration (such as Eclectic and even Klingon Wicca!) that Gardner might not recognize as springing from his personal vision. But if it's true that Gerald Gardner's writing and teaching spawned many spiritual children, he could also boast of a fair number of grandchildren, great-grandchildren, and more than a few distant cousins! Save for those who claim an ancestral or cultural "old tradition" equivalent to the one that Gardner himself reconstructed, almost every other form of modern neo-Pagan Witchcraft has assimilated at least some of the basic elements of Gardnerian-style Wicca.

The British anti-Witchcraft laws were repealed in 1951. Soon after that, Gardner's books, along with those of Sybil Leek and others, reached an eager American audience already intrigued by such works as Margaret Murray's *The Witch Cult in Western Europe* (1921). Some men and women who would later emerge as literary or inspirational leaders of a blossoming movement set sail for England to seek training in this "new" old Craft. What they returned with, they shared with others. Soon a wave of Pagan believers began to emerge.

For almost twenty years, small but growing numbers of practicing Wiccans remained hidden from public view. Abiding by the oath of secrecy as recorded in "The Old Laws," groups interacted primarily with others of similar beliefs or lineage. The available documents were open only to those who had been initiated into a proper Wiccan coven, and the contents of these papers and books remained a closely guarded secret. Then along came the seventies.

Wounded by the Vietnam War and jaded by governmental hypocrisy, there seemed to be a restless longing in the hearts and spirits of a generation. They wanted something different. They wanted something new. What they found was based upon something old. Two books, both published on October 31, 1979, ushered in a new decade and spawned a revolution in spiritual experience. *The Spiral Dance* by Starhawk and Margot Adler's *Drawing Down the Moon* reintroduced the concepts of Goddess worship and ancient Pagan religious rituals. As interest in these subjects continued to develop, Pagans searched for more information about the roots, traditions, and origins of their faith. Their quest led them back, once again, to Gerald Gardner and *Witchcraft Today*.

The rest, as they say, is history. In truth, the rest actually *made* history. The spiritual life of the modern world would never be the same again. From those first few books arose an entire publishing industry devoted to Pagan interests. In time, some of these authors would create their own new Wiccan-based traditions. Scott Cunningham's *Wicca: A Guide for the Solitary Practitioner* and *Seax Wicca* by Raymond Buckland not only reformatted many traditional Wiccan rituals and concepts, they may also have helped to redefine what it means to be Wiccan today. What Gerald Gardner might think of solitary Wicca, we cannot know. Nor can we guess his reactions to the many labels and myriad guises that Wicca wears today. He might be thrilled. He might be surprised. He might not be entirely pleased with all of these new variations, but I daresay he would be fascinated—and impressed.

And he would most definitely have a website.

As of this writing, The Witches' Voice website alone lists over twenty thousand individuals across the globe who self-identify as Wiccans. And for every one of those, there are probably dozens more who are not listed. There are also 3,276 covens and group listings and over 685 Pagan shops. While the actual number of practicing Wiccans is unrecorded, less and less are the official numbers-crunchers, media reporters, and the Pagan practitioners themselves shying away from the word *millions*. We are, in this twenty-first century reality, everywhere.

All over the world, local groups are forming; private and public circles as well as rituals are being scheduled. Events held in celebration of the eight Wiccan Sabbats are listed in many newspapers right alongside an upcoming Baptist convention or a Lutheran potluck supper. Wiccan and Pagan religious figures serve as chaplains in prisons and at hospitals. Many interfaith councils now include one or more Wiccan members. Wiccan and Pagan clergy offer invocations at public meetings. The U.S. Air Force and Army allow for the Wiccan or Pagan designation to be placed on dog tags. Pagan student groups gather on many campuses. Many books are now being written for that growing youth audience. Numerous magazines like *Insight* and *Youthwork* report that Wicca is a major interest for girls in their teens. There are even novels and films with Wiccan heroes and heroines. Wicca has gone mainstream.

The influx of new seekers shows no immediate signs of abatement. This movement toward a very open and often derivative Wicca is here for us to examine—and argue over. It has become a source of considerable controversy and debate within Wiccan communities. Is the only true Wiccan a Gardnerian Wiccan? Or is Wicca now whatever the myriad of those who use the title say it is?

What are we to make of this new and very public Wicca? What would Gerald do? He'd probably log into a Pagan chat room or message board. He might even have one himself. There are literally thousands of such Web-based communication vehicles on the Internet today. Wiccans can connect with others across the world and discuss issues like the above questions and much more. And debate the issues, they do. It's ironic, but probably also appropriate, that so many decades after the publication of *Witchcraft Today*, we find ourselves back somewhere close to the beginning. We asked, "What is Wicca?" when first we heard of the word, and many of us are asking the same question today.

So, what is Wicca? Is it still the small, somewhat guarded, and intimate coven-structured initiatory mystery sect, much the same as it was when Gardner himself first penned the words of the rites into his Book of Shadows? Or is it the worldwide phenomenon practiced by perhaps millions of people and in almost as many ways?

Wicca today is both of these and more: It is a chosen faith. It is a mystery tradition. It is one of the fastest growing religions in the world. It is guarded by some and flaunted by others. It is struggling; it is burgeoning. It is becoming. It has arrived. And it will survive into the foreseeable future. For, more than just a book filled with pages of pretty prose or a set of instructions on how to become a Witch, Gerald Gardner left us, in his works, both a gift and a vision.

His gift to us—summoned forth by whatever means and from whatever sources—is a legacy. It comes from times long past and continues to move us and inspire many to come forth and to embrace again those Ancient Ones Whom he called the God and the Goddess. And his vision that the Old Ones and those who called upon their names would once again be heard has come to pass. The many names of the Gods and the Goddesses of old already spring, soaring and reverent, from the lips of hundreds of thousands of people every day. And undoubtedly from the lips of even more tomorrow.

Whether this is what Gardner intended, this is what Wicca *is*. From one small group of people meeting in secret, Wicca has grown into a worldwide faith of increasing relevance, recognition, and power. And chances are pretty good that if Old Gerald were still here today, he would simply wink at such questions and so leave us to believe (or not) that this very sort of "strange mystical experience" is exactly what he had planned all along.

LOOKING FORWARD:
GARDNER'S HUNCHES

BY JUDY HARROW

THE ORIGINAL edition of *Witchcraft Today* did not contain an index. Part of my preparation for this reissue was to create one. I did this because it was the easiest way for me to see which topics were most important or interesting to Gardner himself—the subjects he kept returning to throughout the book. In the half century since 1954, a great many more books have been written on the topics that fascinated Gardner, books that I like to think he would have enjoyed and used. What follows are my comments on a few areas that I believe are important, and a few of my favorite books about each one.

CELTS AND DRUIDS

The Celtic peoples were the earliest inhabitants of the British Isles to leave us a literature, and their verbal legacy is mythic, poetic, evocative. Their visual arts and musical traditions are equally compelling. Accordingly, we tend to think of Celtic culture as the oldest and most authentic layer of our own, and seek our models there. For example, many North American Witches choose Circle names from Celtic legends or address their devotions to Celtic deities.

Most of us base our annual ritual cycle (the "Wheel of the Year") on the seasonal cycle in Britain. So we honor our cultural roots but at the same time risk distancing ourselves from the spirits of the land in which we live, particularly if the local climate and ecology are markedly different from those of Britain. Obviously, it's more problematic in California or Australia than it is in New England.

The very heart of Celtic spirituality is creating and maintaining a right relationship between the Tribe and the Land. If we keep this issue central, we may be guided into creative adaptations of Celtic myth and ritual, instead of anachronistic and unauthentic rote role-playing.

Celtic society was highly stratified. The Druids were a Celtic priestly order. Several reconstructionist Druid groups exist today, both in Britain and in North America.

To learn more about Celtic spirituality:

Carr-Gomm, Philip, ed. *The Druid Renaissance: The Voice of Druidry Today.* New York: Thorsons, 1998.

Cowan, Tom. *Fire in the Head: Shamanism and the Celtic Spirit.* New York: HarperCollins, 1993.

Davidson, H. R. Ellis. *Myths and Symbols in Pagan Europe: Early Scandinavian and Celtic Religions.* Syracuse, NY: Syracuse University Press, 1988; reissued Palm Springs, CA: Scientists of New Atlantis, 2001.

Green, Miranda. *The World of the Druids.* London: Thames & Hudson, 1997.

Kondratiev, Alexei. *The Apple Branch: A Path to Celtic Ritual.* New York: Citadel, 2003.

Piggott, Stuart. *The Druids.* New York: Thames & Hudson, 1985.

Rees, Alwyn and Brinley. *Celtic Heritage.* New York: Thames & Hudson, 1989.

DANCE

Doreen Valiente, one of Gardner's High Priestesses, says this about dance:

> "Dancing has a very important magical effect upon people. . . . A group of people dancing in harmony together are of one mind, and this is essential to magical work. Their mood can be excited or calmed by varying the pace of the dance. In fact, a state of light hypnosis can be induced by magical forms of dancing; or people can achieve a state of ecstasy, which in its original form is *ex-stasis,* 'being outside oneself.'
>
> "That is, the everyday world is left behind . . . and the magical realms open. The old witch dances helped people to attain this experience, and it was the excitement and enjoyment of the wild dancing, by night in the open air or in some deserted ruin or secret rendezvous, that was one of the main attractions of the Old Religion. . . .
>
> ". . . A dance can be a prayer, an invocation, an ecstasy, or a spell. It is world-old and world-wide magic."

Gardner knew the importance of dance from his interactions with tribal peoples. He was probably also familiar with Sufi-style trance dancing through his acquaintance with Idries Shah. Since his time, interest in dance has been growing. A new movement, called Sacred Circle Dance, which uses rhythmic bodily movement to alter consciousness, emerged at the Findhorn spiritual community in Scotland and has spread quietly and rapidly from there.

To learn more about ritual dance:

Bourguignon, Erika. "Trance Dance." *Dance Perspectives* #35 (Autumn, 1968). New York: Dance Perspectives Foundation, 1968. (Note: This entire issue of *Dance Perspectives* is devoted to Bourguignon's essay.)

Frances, Lynn, and Richard Bryant-Jefferies. *The Sevenfold Circle: Self Awareness in Dance.* Findhorn, Scotland: Findhorn Press, 1998, pp. 40–64.

Jones, Evan John, with Chas Clifton. *Sacred Mask; Sacred Dance.* St.Paul: Llewellyn, 1997.

Lewis, Samuel L. *Spiritual Dances and Walks.* Fairfax, CA: Peaceworks, 1990. (This is a book about Sufi dancing.)

Roth, Gabrielle. *Sweat Your Prayers: Movement as Spiritual Practice.* New York: Putnam, 1998.

Stewart, Iris J. *Sacred Woman, Sacred Dance: Awakening Spirituality Through Movement & Ritual.* Rochester, VT: Inner Traditions, 2000.

Wosien, Maria-Gabriele. *Sacred Dance: Encounter with the Gods.* New York: Thames & Hudson, 1986.

The God

Although what is most noticeable and different about Witchcraft is Goddess worship, Gardnerian Witches also give honor to the God. Other British Traditional Witches, members of traditions closely related to our own, do so as well. Insofar as our religion is Earth-based and fertility-oriented, we recognize that either gender is sterile without the other, at least on the physical plane.

The great Horned God of the forest has been conflated with the Biblical devil, but nowhere in the Bible is the devil described as having horns. When two religions come into conflict, polytheisms tend to have their pantheons intermarry. Monotheistic cults, lacking this option, instead demonize the other people's Gods. Our God is not anybody's devil. Rather He is the image of the proud, free male, His horns those of the mighty stag. He is Robin MacArt and John Barleycorn and Jack in the Green. He is the shining sun, the provider and protector of the Tribe. He brings joy to the Goddess and to the people.

To learn more about the God:

Anderson, William. *Green Man: The Archetype of Our Oneness with the Earth.* San Francisco: Harper Collins, 1990.

Bolen, Jean Shinoda. *Gods in Everyman.* San Francisco: Harper & Row, 1989.

Farrar, Janet and Stewart. *The Witches' God: Lord of the Dance.* Custer, WA: Phoenix, 1989.

Jackson, Nigel. *Masks of Misrule: The Horned God and His Cult in Europe.* Chieveley, UK: Capall Bann, 1996.

Matthews, John. *The Green Man: Spirit of Nature.* York Beach, ME: Red Wheel/Weiser, 2002.

Rowan, John. *The Horned God.* New York: Routledge & Kegan Paul, 1987.

THE GODDESS

Our Lady is best known as Mother Nature or Mother Earth, although people have given Her countless other names. She is the soul of nature, who gives life to the universe. All that lives comes from Her generous womb. All that dies returns to Her as a drop of rain returns, at long last, to the ocean.

Through the long centuries of suppression, we have forgotten the sacredness of Earth. We think of Her as an object for use rather than as a living being with intrinsic and sacred value. Consequently, She is in mortal danger, and because we are part of Her, because our lives are utterly dependent on Hers, humankind is in danger as well. Perhaps this is why we feel the need to reaffirm our connection with Her right now, why Goddess worship is coming again to the fore. Please understand that there are very many more Goddess worshippers than there are Witches. We have much in common but also many differences in our approach. The "Goddess Movement" can best be understood as the place where neo-Paganism overlaps with feminist spirituality.

This dramatic upwelling of interest in the feminine divine has also generated a remarkable amount of good writing about the Goddess and about Goddesses. It was difficult for me to select a short list from among the many, many worthwhile books that are now available. Please note that every one of the books mentioned below was published after Gerald Gardner's death.

To learn more about the Goddess:

Bolen, Jean Shinoda. *Goddesses in Everywoman*. San Francisco: Harper & Row, 1993.

Christ, Carol. *Rebirth of the Goddess*. Boulder, CO: Perseus, 2000.

————, and Judith Plaskow, eds. *Womanspirit Rising: A Feminist Reader in Religion*. San Francisco: Harper & Row, 1979. (This anthology set the course of feminist theology. Carol Christ's essay "Why Women Need the Goddess" is an important key to understanding Goddess worship.)

Davidson, H. R. Ellis. *Roles of the Northern Goddess*. London: Routledge, 1998.

Downing, Christine. *The Goddess: Mythological Images of the Feminine*. New York: Continuum, 1996. (This book focuses on the Goddesses of ancient Greece. Even if you are not particularly drawn to the Greek pantheon, it is worth reading for the model it offers of how to feel into the connections between mythic portrayals and your own life experience.)

Woolger, Jennifer and Roger. *The Goddess Within*. New York: Ballantine, 1989.

Indigenous Spirituality

Gardner's life of travel gave him wide opportunities to experience the spiritual practices of indigenous peoples. He was open-minded and curious, so instead of huddling with other imperial officials in self-imposed ghettos, he visited, befriended, witnessed, experienced, and learned. Later, he brought these rich memories back to his work in Britain. Yet, despite his progressiveness, he was of course bound by cultural context. Is there some set of hereditary talents for spirituality or magic, talents best preserved among some "elder races"? In *Witchcraft Today*, Gardner seems to think so; it was a paradigm of his time, and we have no idea how Gardner would weigh in with current information regarding the nature/nurture debate continuing to haunt the fields of psychology and pedagogy. Gardner's inquiry, nevertheless, was real and serious: He sought to learn the spiritual techniques and lore of indigenous people as well as honor his own cultural roots. He wanted to learn.

Below, I am including a book on Malaysian spirit shamanism, the indigenous tradition with which Gardner had the most sustained contact, and which has some intriguing similarities to contemporary Gardnerian-based Witchcraft. He was also fascinated with Voodoo, mentioning it again and again in *Witchcraft Today*. Voodoo is a robust, vibrant indigenous religion, which lately has inspired some fine writing.

To learn more about indigenous spirituality:

Brown, Karen McCarthy. *Mama Lola: A Vodou Priestess in Brooklyn.* Berkeley: University of California Press, 2001.

Cosentino, Donald J., ed. *Sacred Arts of Hatian Vodou.* Los Angeles: UCLA Fowler Museum, 1995.

Deren, Maya. *Divine Horsemen: The Living Gods of Haiti.* Kingston, NY: McPherson, 1984. (An earlier edition of this book is in the Gardner Collection.)

Laderman, Carol. *Taming the Wind of Desire: Psychology, Medicine and Aesthetics in Malay Shamanistic Performance.* Berkeley: University of California Press, 1991.

Metraux, Alfred. *Voodoo in Haiti.* New York: Schocken, 1989.

Teish, Luisah. *Jambalaya: The Natural Woman's Book of Personal Charms and Practical Rituals.* New York: Harper, 1988.

INITIATION

Initiation is a ritual of passage. Rituals of passage both make and mark major changes in a person's life. Effective rituals make change because they are powerful means of communication with the person's deepest mind and with the Otherworld. They mark change because they formally install the person into a new role or status in his or her community. It's easy to see this dual function in the passage ritual that is most familiar in our society, a wedding. There, the couple exchange sacred vows with one another, consecrating their love bond, after which they assume a new, and often more adult, status in their community. Similarly with a Witch's initiation ritual: The candidate is both committed to the priestly service of the Ancient Gods and admitted to membership in a coven and tradition.

British Traditional Witches use a three-degree system that is roughly comparable to the sequential roles of apprentice, journeyman, and master in the old craft guilds or bachelor, master, and doctor in modern academia. Since our initiations do bring the person into the role of priestess or priest, we do our best to conduct rituals that are powerful, beautiful, and spiritually transformative. If you seek and accept initiation, your life will never again be the same.

To learn more about initiation:

Eliade, Mircea. *Rites and Symbols of Initiation: The Mysteries of Birth and Rebirth.* Woodstock, CT: Spring, 1994.

LaFontaine, J. S. *Initiation: Ritual Drama and Secret Knowledge Across the World.* New York: Viking Penguin, 1985.

Meade, Michael J. *Men and the Water of Life: Initiation and the Tempering of Men.* New York: HarperCollins, 1994.

Perera, Sylvia Brinton. *Descent to the Goddess: A Way of Initiation for Women.* Toronto: Inner City, 1991.

Shorter, Bani. *An Image Darkly Forming: Women and Initiation.* London: Routledge & Kegan Paul, 1987.

Turner, Victor. "The Liminal Period in Rites of Passage." In Mahdi, Louise Carus, Steven Foster, and Meredith Little, eds., *Betwixt and Between: Patterns of Masculine and Feminine Initiation* (LaSalle, IL: Open Court, 1987), pp. 3–19. (Note: If you can only read one thing about initiation, I recommend this essay! The rest of the anthology is also very worthwhile.)

SHAMANISM

The word *shamanism* does not appear in *Witchcraft Today*. Instead, Gardner uses equivalent terms like *palingenesis* as he talks about similar phenomena. Simply put, a shaman is one who dreams, or trances, or explores the Otherworld in service to the People. Because they develop special skills in trancework and inner exploration, shamans are often described as technicians of the Sacred.

For some years now, there has been a great deal of popular interest in indigenous people and their lifeways, including shamanic spiritual practices. It's a trend, maybe even a fad, but it has resulted in many good books being written and much more information becoming available. Far from disparaging a cultural fad, we should be grateful for the help it provides to us.

Witches read these books too. Much of what we read is intriguing, some of it hauntingly familiar. We see that shamanism is widespread, a primal religious response. Logically, there is no reason for Europe to be left out. From this viewpoint, we begin to perceive a sequence within European culture as well: the cave paintings of

Altamira and Lascaux, so like shamanic art elsewhere; records of trance and oracular practices fading out earlier in the "classical" south than in the "barbarian" north; Witch-trial accusations of practices that are physically impossible but are also normal trance experiences like flying or animal transformations. We are reclaiming our own heritage, the shamanic lifeways and practices of Europe, that were dormant for so long. Because of extensive, perhaps even total, breaks in transmission, we need to borrow, improvise, and invent in order to properly piece it together. For us, information about shamanic practices from elsewhere is a precious resource.

To learn more about shamanism:

Blain, Jenny. *Nine Worlds of Seid-Magic.* London: Routledge, 2002.

Cowan, Tom. *Shamanism as a Spiritual Practice for Daily Life.* Freedom, CA: Crossing Press, 1996.

Eliade, Mircea. *Shamanism: Archaic Techniques of Ecstasy.* Princeton, NJ: Princeton University Press, 1964; reissued by Viking Penguin, 1989.

Halifax, Joan. *Shamanic Voices: A Survey of Visionary Narratives.* New York: Penguin, 1991.

Harner, Michael. *The Way of the Shaman: A Guide to Power and Healing.* New York: Harper, 1990. (This one was the trend-setter.)

Hutton, Ronald. *Shamans: Siberian Spirituality and the Western Imagination.* London: Hambledon and London, 2001.

Larsen, Stephen. *The Shaman's Doorway.* Rochester, VT: Inner Traditions, 1998.

Lewis, Ioan M. *Ecstatic Religion: A Study of Shamanism and Spirit Possession.* London: Routledge, 2003.

Noel, Daniel C. *The Soul of Shamanism: Western Fantasies, Imaginal Realities.* New York: Continuum, 1997.

SPELLCRAFT *(projective magic)*

Witches make magic: We believe that we can project our active will out into the world to create change. This is probably the most intriguing and exotic thing about us, far more strange to a modern, secular worldview than even Goddess worship. Witches heal.

Some define magic as the art of causing change in accordance with will. Others, myself included, prefer to define it as the art of changing consciousness in accordance with will. But to change consciousness is to change behavior, and to change behavior is to change response. So perhaps the difference between the two definitions is not so great after all. What matters is results.

I'm including some books that approach magic traditionally and others that grow out of very current science—they're finally catching up with us. Psychoneuroimmunology (the study of how the mind, *psycho*, working through the nervous system, *neuro*, affects the immune system, *immunology*, to promote healing) is a young science. It is now explicating and validating many ancient methods of healing, such as therapeutic touch and active imagination. Does it sound familiar—how changing consciousness in accordance with will creates measurable, physical change? Some would call that magic.

To learn more about spellcraft:

Achterberg, Jeanne. *Imagery in Healing: Shamanism and Modern Medicine*. Boston: Shambhala, 2002.

————, Barbara Dossey, and Leslie Kolkmeier. *Rituals of Healing: Using Imagery for Health and Wellness*. New York: Bantam, 1994.

Bonewits, P. E. I. *Real Magic*. York Beach, ME: Red Wheel/Weiser, 1989.

Krieger, Dolores. *Therapeutic Touch as Transpersonal Healing*. New York: Lantern, 2002. (Note: Dolores Krieger earned her Ph.D. by documenting the importance of therapeutic touch in nursing.)

McLelland, Lilith. *Spellcraft: A Primer for the Young Magician*. Chicago: Eschaton, 1998.

Reid, Sian. "As I Do Will, So Mote It Be: Magic as Metaphor in Neo-Pagan Witchcraft." In Lewis, James R., ed., *Magical Religion and Modern Witchcraft* (Albany: State University of New York Press, 1996), pp. 141–167. (This anthology also contains several other worthwhile essays.)

Wood, Robin. *When, Why . . . If*. Dearborn, MI: Livingtree, 1996. (Note: This book is not about the techniques of spellcraft; it is about ethics. Those who believe that magic really does cause change are well-advised to think through the ethical considerations involved.)

BEYOND GARDNER'S WILDEST DREAMS:
PAGAN RELIGIOUS STUDIES

Gardner must be grinning in his grave! He was, after all, something of an amateur anthropologist himself, with well-respected publications on subjects like the Malaysian keris knife, even though he never attended a university. Since his time, our society insists much more on formal academic credentials. It was inevitable that, with most younger Pagans going to college, many of us followed academic careers. Some of us chose to make our religion, the heart of our lives, into the focus of our studies. And some non-Pagan scholars also became interested in us as a cultural phenomenon of growing importance. In both the United States and Great Britain, we are now seeing the emergence of Pagan religious studies as an independent sub-field.

The book list below was compiled by Chas S. Clifton, a pioneer of Pagan academics. Chas is a professor at the University of Southern Colorado, convener of the Nature Religion Scholars Network, and most recently, co-editor of a new series of scholarly books on Pagan Studies from AltaMira Press. The list is included here by his gracious permission.

Nature religion, history and theory:

Albanese, Catherine. *Nature Religion in America: From the Algonkian Indians to the New Age.* Chicago: University of Chicago Press, 1990.
Chidester, David, and Edwart T. Linenthal, eds. *American Sacred Space.* Bloomington: Indiana University Press, 1995.

Contemporary Paganism, nature-centered religions:

Berger, Helen. *A Community of Witches: Contemporary Neo-Paganism and Witchcraft in the United States.* Columbia: University of South Carolina Press, 1999.
Blain, Jenny. *Nine Worlds of Seid-Magic.* London: Routledge, 2002.
Bloch, Jon P. *New Spirituality, Self, and Belonging: How New Agers and Neo-Pagans Talk About Themselves.* Westport, CT: Praeger, 1998.
Greenwood, Susan. *Magic and the Otherworld.* Berg, 2000.
Griffin, Wendy, ed. *Daughters of the Goddess.* Walnut Creek, CA: AltaMira Press, 2000.
Harvey, Graham. *Contemporary Paganism: Listening People, Speaking Earth.* New York: New York University Press, 1997.
———, and Charlotte Hardman, eds. *Paganism Today: Wiccans, Druids, the Goddess and Ancient Earth Traditions for the Twenty-first Century.* London: Thorsons, 1996.
Hutton, Ronald. *The Stations of the Sun: A History of the Ritual Year in Britain.* Oxford: Oxford University Press, 1996.
———. *The Triumph of the Moon: A History of Modern Pagan Witchcraft.* Oxford: Oxford University Press, 2000.

Hume, Lynn. *Witchcraft and Paganism in Australia.* Carlton South, Victoria: Melbourne University Press, 1997.

Keenan, Tanya E. *Living in the Broom Closet: Hiding Neo-Paganism in the Culture of Confession.* M.A. thesis, University of South Florida, 1998.

Lewis, James R., ed. *Magical Religion and Modern Witchcraft.* Albany: State University of New York Press, 1996.

Orion, Loretta. *Never Again the Burning Times: Paganism Revived.* Prospect Heights, IL: Waveland Press, 1995.

Pearson, Joanne, Richard Roberts, and Geoffrey Samuel, eds. *Nature Religion Today: Paganism in the Modern World.* Edinburgh: Edinburgh University Press, 1998.

Pike, Sarah. *Earthly Bodies, Magical Selves.* Berkeley: University of California Press, 2001.

Raphael, Melissa. *Introducing Thealogy: Discourse on the Goddess.* Sheffield: Sheffield Academic Press, 1999.

———. *Thealogy and Embodiment: The Post-Patriarchal Reconstruction of Female Sacrality.* Sheffield: Sheffield Academic Press, 1996.

York, Michael. *Pagan Theology: Paganism as a World Religion.* New York: New York University Press, 2003.

For more on the Nature Religion Scholars Network, visit their website at chass.colostate-pueblo.edu/natrel/

WICCAN HISTORY

Our history is a matter of debate, as we try to sort out what is objective fact from what is more properly understood as constituting our myths of origins. On one level, history doesn't matter at all, if what we do helps us grow in spiritual connection to the Ancient Gods of Nature; on another, history is endlessly fascinating and helps us to understand ourselves. These books and articles will help you understand more about the historical issues before us.

Adler, Margot. *Drawing Down the Moon: Witches, Druids, Goddess-Worshippers, and Other Pagans in America Today,* rev. ed. Boston: Beacon, 1986.

Ashcroft-Nowicki, Dolores, ed. *The Forgotten Mage: The Magical Lectures of Colonel C.R.F. Seymour.* Wellingborough, Northamptonshire, UK: Aquarian, 1986. (Seymour was one of Gardner's most important precursors.)

Baker, James W. "White Witches: Historic Fact and Romantic Fantasy." In Lewis, James R., ed., *Magical Religion and Modern Witchcraft*

(Albany: State University of New York Press, 1996), pp. 171–92. (This anthology also contains several other worthwhile essays.)

Bracelin, J. L. *Gerald Gardner: Witch*. London: Octagon, 1960.

Gardner, Gerald B. *The Meaning of Witchcraft*. London: Aquarian, 1959.

Ginzburg, Carlo. *Ecstasies: Deciphering the Witches' Sabbat*. New York: Pantheon, 1991.

Hutton, Ronald. *The Triumph of the Moon: A History of Modern Pagan Witchcraft*. Oxford: Oxford University Press, 2000.

Murray, Margaret A. *The God of the Witches*. New York: Oxford University Press, 1992.

———. *The Witch-Cult in Western Europe*. New York: Oxford University Press, 1971.

Russell, Jeffrey B. *A History of Witchcraft: Sorcerers, Heretics and Pagans*. New York: Thames & Hudson, 1980. (This is actually a history of people's ideas about those topics.)

Starhawk. *The Spiral Dance*. San Francisco: Harper & Row, 1989.

Valiente, Doreen. *The Rebirth of Witchcraft*. London: Hale, 1989.

———. *An ABC of Witchcraft Past and Present*. New York: St. Martin's, 1973.

York, Michael. *Pagan Theology: Paganism as a World Religion*. New York: New York University Press, 2003.

And visit www.geraldgardner.com.

THE WICCAN FUTURE: A CAMPUS
VIEWPOINT

BY TARA NELSEN

I WAS recently invited to speak about Wicca and Paganism at a local high school class on ethics and religious diversity. This town is a small community, deep in the Bible Belt. The class was created in response to a community-wide controversy surrounding the posting of the Ten Commandments inside the public school. I felt it was an opportunity to tell local youth the truth about Paganism and to express the fact that there are many different religious beliefs held in their own community.

"How many of you had heard of Wicca or Paganism before taking this class?" I watched in amazement as more than half the class raised their hands. It wasn't like this when I started on my path. This particular community was not only predominately Christian but very fundamentalist and right-wing in their beliefs. These students were raised to be close-minded and had less than average exposure to the diversity of the world. That was my presumption. Over the years, something had changed.

I became interested in witchcraft, Paganism, and what I later found out was called Wicca over fourteen years ago, when I was a little younger than these students. Nearly half of my life has been spent exploring and experiencing the Craft and dedicating myself to it, and telling people the truth about our ways: how we, as Pagans, are not evil; that we are not bad; and that we are in fact very similar to most everyone else out there! We, too, have jobs, kids, pets, hobbies, loves, dreams, and more. Yet, despite the promise of a room full of students acknowledging Wicca with raised hands, I'm not naïve enough to think that the battle for tolerance has been won. I have seen what time can do, though, and I believe that acceptance can happen in my lifetime. That is part of why I fight.

As a graduate student, in the midst of my college career, the campus is a powerful place to examine the evolving Pagan culture and create a new reality. In the last five years I have gone from having to explain what the five-pointed star around my neck means to having folks come up to me, point at my necklace, and say, "Hey, are you Wiccan? Great . . . that is so cool!" I have been able to feel safe placing Pagan-themed bumper stickers on my car, not fearing that they will be damaged, which was once a reality for me. We are no longer quite so strange, mysterious, or scary. We have become familiar, almost normal. We no longer are just sardonic little news features at Halloween.

Campus is a place of diversity where students are trained to question, to search, and to look for new ways to grow and change as individuals. It is a place where we can change ourselves. Like good colleges anywhere, my campus is a nurturing place centered around change, with ever-increasing local college and university Pagan groups forming that are easily found on-campus or connected to over the Internet. Such groups support their members' spiritual development, and also let other students of all religions know who we really are: their neighbors, "normal" people who also care.

Our path is now more accepted, safer—yet not without responsibility. As we become better known, we also become more superficially attractive to those who do not want to do the hard work of magick and Spirit: the inner exploration of our beliefs and our actions, and how we as individuals and members of society connect to the Divine. Allowed to be recognized and understood, the people of the Craft must naturally change in such an environment, and they will make room for new and different ideas, practices, beliefs, and energy. I believe, however, that students, thriving in such places, will not find stasis but instead produce new Starhawks, new Scott Cunninghams and Dorothy Morrisons . . . maybe even new Gerald Gardners.

There is another population that will perhaps have an even greater, and most certainly longer, influence on the future of the Craft . . . the kids. Adolescents and teenagers are finding Wicca as fast, if not faster, than college students and adults. They are making the same dedications to this path as the older generations. It is our responsibility as elders, teachers, guides, and fellow seekers to allow the next generation to learn the ways of the Craft and to help them understand the deeper meanings and history of our traditions beyond love spells and glamour magick. We must be involved with providing *them* safe places. It is our responsibility to support them as they step out and raise their voices in public. We must allow them to do work, too, must pass the flame to them and provide a foundation, even when we disagree with a method or presentation style, even when their participation sparks controversy.

The future is forming. Reality is always changing. We are building our future and our reality at this moment. It has only been a short time, a mere blink in the eye of history, that Witches have been safe to openly express who we are and what we do. Our future is open for so much more. I hope it will bring more public education about our ways; more success in our fight for freedom of religion so that we can choose our path and celebrate our traditions; more groups large and small, public and private, to increase people's choices; and more of the community networking that keeps us aware of the changes and the growth of our religion. I also hope to see less infighting. We have too much to fight for and to defend ourselves against to waste the energy fighting with each other.

The future of our Craft is in the hands of the adolescent picking up her first book of spells. The future is in the minds of the teenager and his friends casting their first Circle. The future is in the eyes and voices of the campus group chanting as they walk through the student union. The future is in the hearts of women celebrating their moon blood. The future is in the arms of the woman honoring her cronehood. The future is in the dreams of the newbies and in the dreams of the elders who watch as the future emerges. We are all children of the Gods. We can make our will manifest. The future is us. Let's make it magick!

BLESSED BE!

ABOUT THE CONTRIBUTORS

JUDY HARROW, a Gardnerian High Priestess, has led Proteus Coven since 1980. She invites you to visit the Proteus Coven website at www.draknet.com/proteus. Judy earned her master's degree in counseling from the City College of New York in 1979. Her lifelong passion has been to explore and explain the many deep connections between psychology and spirituality. She is currently president-elect of the New Jersey Association for Spiritual, Ethical and Religious Values in Counseling, and chair of the Pastoral Counseling program at Cherry Hill Seminary.

Judy has written two books: *Wicca Covens* (Citadel, 1999), an introduction to group dynamics for coven leaders and members, and *Spiritual Mentoring* (ECW, 2002), an exploration of the sacred process of guiding the spiritual development of others. She also edited and contributed to *Devoted to You* (Citadel, 2003), an anthology about creating a personal relationship to specific Pagan Deities through study and devotional practice.

Judy would like to dedicate her work on this fiftieth anniversary reissue of Gardner's book to three great women who contributed to Gardner's life and work:

> Donna, his wife, who gave him space to pursue interests she did not share.
>
> Dafo, his first working partner, who helped him plant the garden.
>
> Doreen, who weeded and pruned, and added a few good seeds of her own.

Blessed be their memories in all the Worlds!

RONALD HUTTON is professor of history at Bristol University, one of the world's leading authorities on Pagan history, and author of *The Rise and Fall of Merrie England, Stations of the Sun, The Triumph of the Moon,* and *Shamans.*

WREN WALKER is the co-founder/chairperson of The Witches' Voice, Inc. (www.witchvox.com) and the author of many of the basic documents posted on the Witches' Voice site. Speaking as a lifelong Witch and a social and civil rights activist, she has been interviewed on numerous radio programs, television shows, and for many of the major newspapers. Wren facilitates workshops on Pagan rights issues at festivals throughout the country and provides a news clipping service called, Wren's Nest (www.witchvox.com/xwrensnest.html). She shares a home with TWV co-founder and husband Fritz Jung and their two kitties, Ruby and Dixie. When time permits, her hobbies include reading, writing poetry/song lyrics, and drawing cartoons—but if there happens to be an original Godzilla movie on TV, everything else goes on hold!

TARA NELSEN, an eclectic Witch and Pagan, has been studying Paganism and the Craft for over fourteen years, nearly half her life. She has a B.A. in liberal arts, with minors in environmental studies, philosophy, and women's studies, and is now working on a master's degree in health education. Tara founded Universal Spirituality, a local pagan discussion group, and is co-founder and facilitator of SIPA—the Southern Illinois Pagan Alliance. Tara lives in Illinois with nine cats, a dog, a husband, and a great garden. She is part owner of the only Pagan bookstore in Southern Illinois, New Ages/Other Worlds.

INDEX
for Gerald B. Gardner's *Witchcraft Today*

broomstick (riding pole), 34, 35, 53–54

Celts (linguistic and cultural group, once widespread in Europe, now living in Brittany, Cornwall, Ireland, the Isle of Man, Scotland, and Wales), 37–38, 42, 130

Circle (consecrated space, within which Witches meet for worship), 26–27, 29, 44–48, 77

clairvoyance (acute intuitive perception, experienced visually), 21, 28, 126–127

dance, 15–16, 20, 22, 46, 53–54, 90–92, 99, 110–111, 115, 123, 141–142, 145

Druid (member of an ancient Celtic priestly order), 36–38, 44, 48

fairy (magical being—perhaps a land spirit, perhaps a member of an older indigenous people—now living in remote areas and on the fringes of the community), 17, 39, 56–57, 59, 60, 64, 116

familiars (closely-bonded animal companions), 65, 139, 143–145 [Note: The picture of a male Witch with his familiar that Margaret Murray describes in the excerpt, pp. 143–144, is reproduced in the book *An ABC of Witchcraft Past and Present* by Doreen Valiente (New York: St Martin's, 1973) in the photo section between pages 192 and 193.]

Garter, Order of, 119–121

gender issues, 31–33, 43–44, 64–65, 75, 115

God (see also ROBIN), 32, 40, 49, 74, 135–136, 145

Goddess, 32, 38, 41–42, 62, 64–65

Grail (cauldron, chalice), 71, 77, 79–80, 125–126 [To learn more, see Matthews, John, ed., *Sources of the Grail* (Hudson, NY: Lindisfarne, 1997).]